"To be effective in living and serving others with honor you must be able to keep your commitments. This requires a high degree of being prepared to be accountable and everyday taking the right actions. Lee Ellis provides you with the most robust how-to framework and skills required for keeping yourself and others on track to perform at the highest level."

Hugh Massie,
President and Founder – DNA Behavior International

"In his book *Engage with Honor*, Lee provides valuable lessons in leadership learned from the world's toughest 'leadership lab,' The Hanoi Hilton. His models and guidelines totally encompasses the word integrity in each example which is essential to a good and courageous leader. Another great read by my old friend. "

Gene Smith,
Former Vietnam POW; Past National President and Chairman of the Board, Air Force Association

"Once again, Lee has integrated his very personal life experiences as a Vietnam POW to provide very pertinent and valuable leadership lessons applicable for any leader!! I couldn't have anticipated the significant lessons embedded in the Courageous Accountability Model. Throughout the entire book, the lessons shared served as not only a refresher but a graduate level course in leadership as well."

Carol H. Burrell,
President and CEO, Northeast Georgia Health System

"Highly relevant, clear, and practical, *Engage with Honor* provides leaders with models that enable critical thinking and inspire intentional action. If you desire to lead from heart with courage and accountability, then this is the book to guide you!"

Tami Heim,
President & CEO of Christian Leadership Alliance

ENDORSEMENTS

"Lee Ellis has a powerful story, is a outstanding author, and drives home the message of courageous accountability in a compelling way. Lee aptly observes, and I agree, that 'Accountability is crucial to success' and that 'Wise people welcome the guardrails that accountability provides to keep them on track and avoid going over the cliff.' I would add: Wise ministries also welcome the guardrails. You will want to give this book to your leadership team to positively impact your organization!"

Dan Busby,
President – ECFA

"*Engage with Honor* is a winner all around! Lee Ellis has surpassed his last book, *Leading with Honor,* which I thoroughly treasured and quoted often in my own writings. *Engage with Honor* centers on what is lacking in leadership and organizations today—building a culture of accountability. Accountability is a dimension of leadership that seems to have been lost and it is heartening to see it featured in this book. The principle of engaging with honor and his practical ideas on 'how to do it' should be required reading for all managers, leaders, and those who aspire to be."

Archie B. Carroll, PhD,
Professor of Management Emeritus –
Terry College of Business, University of Georgia

"I can't think of a better person to write about engaging with honor than Lee Ellis. The lessons he learned in 'courageous accountability,' as a combat pilot and POW in Vietnam, permeate this rich and rewarding book. Lee takes his wartime experiences and relates them to what leaders need to do today to powerfully engage those they lead with both honor and accountability. Every leader on every level needs to read this book to engage a culture where honor is lacking and needed more than ever before."

Dick Bruso,
Founder of Heard Above The Noise

"Just like a diamond is known for the 4 C's, honorable leaders are also known for the four C's presented here brilliantly by author Lee Ellis. In this book you will find stories that engage you, insights that transform you, and practical advice you can put in your pocket (or purse) for everyday living. Read it, and find new depth in your own levels of growth."

Laurie Beth Jones,
Author of Jesus, CEO; The Path; *and*
Jesus, Life Coach

"[In *Engage with Honor*], you have taken a challenging time in your life [as a POW] and extracted the very best lessons from it that continue to build layers upon layers to offer greater perspective on our life's full journey. As we all know, it is the challenges in life that most define us. This book gives you a very practical look at how to rise above, embrace, and take ownership of them."

Janine Sijan Rozina,
Sister of Vietnam POW Lance Sijan (MOH) and
Founder of Team Sijan

"In *Engage with Honor: Building a Culture of Courageous Accountability*, Lee Ellis infuses leadership fundamentals with real-life lessons from his military experience and time in captivity as a POW to deliver a highly compelling read for today's business leader. His exploration of accountability and collaboration, two transformative behaviors our organization is trying to accelerate, is enhanced with relevant and discussion-worthy examples. And as with his earlier book, Leading with Honor: Leadership Lessons from the Hanoi Hilton, Lee's philosophy of respect for the individual and integrity (two of Swagelok's core values) are on display for the reader. His experiences should serve as an inspiration to anyone who wants to take their organization to the next level of performance."

Arthur F. Anton,
Chairman, President and CEO, Swagelok Company

ENDORSEMENTS

"Lee artfully tackles the difficult and often misunderstood role of accountability in effective leadership. Building on personal experiences as he's done before, the easy reading format, poignant examples and sage advice make this a must read for both the young and seasoned leader. Courageous Accountability . . . a must in every leader's tool kit."

Lt. Gen. Doug Owens, USAF (Ret.),
National Commander, Order of Daedalians

"There are books that I have read and store on the shelf, and then there are books that I read and keep close so I can refer back time and time again...this is one of those books. Lee's discussion and application of Honor and Accountability as foundational for effective leadership and culture are not theoretical—but proven in refining heat that few leaders today can begin to understand. I would choose to follow a leader that embodies the principles Lee defines. Furthermore . . . this is the kind of leader I aspire to become."

Dan Olson,
Vice President and General Manager, Armament Systems Division – Orbital ATK

"Today's managers are always looking for ways to elevate themselves to be tomorrow's leaders. They are looking for those leadership examples that can inspire. Former POW Air Force Colonel Lee Ellis is just that kind of inspiration. He is one of those leaders who suffered through an unimaginable crucible, the Hanoi Hilton prisoner-of-war camp in North Vietnam, for more than five years. Colonel Ellis' latest book, Engage with Honor: Building a Culture of Courageous Accountability, is a useful book that offers practical -- not just theoretical -- advice on how to authentically link honor and accountability, the critical values that were key to his success."

Taylor Baldwin Kiland,
Co-author of Lessons from the Hanoi Hilton: Six Characteristics of High-Performance Teams, *and* Open Doors: Vietnam POWs Thirty Years Later

"Once again Lee Ellis has created an outstanding book on Leadership, Honor and Accountability. Using his past experiences, both in the military and civilian sector, he provides critical insights and, more importantly, techniques and approaches on 'how to.' A must-read for anyone serious about leading in our world today where honor and accountability are the keys to success!"

Gen. William R. Looney, III, USAF (Ret)

"I'm honored to endorse Lee's book. He is an inspiration to us all. Lee is a highly decorated United States Air Force veteran and POW, and *Engage with Honor* offers necessary and practical leadership lessons that can be easily applied in many different circumstances. Lee relates his own experiences to prepare you to become a better leader."

Bruce N. Whitman,
Immediate Past Co-Chairman, Congressional
Medal of Honor Foundation; Chairman, President
& CEO, FlightSafety International

"I have observed Lee Ellis in leadership roles, and I have read his books on the subject. If there is anyone anywhere who combines both practice and scholarship on the subject equal to Lee, I am certainly not aware of it. All practitioners of the art can learn from this extraordinary man."

Gen. Charles G. Boyd, USAF (Ret.)

ENGAGE WITH HONOR

BUILDING A CULTURE OF
COURAGEOUS ACCOUNTABILITY

LEE ELLIS

Readers should be aware that Internet Web sites mentioned as references or sources for further information may have changed or no longer be available since this book was published.

Published by FreedomStar Media

ISBN (Hardcover Trade Edition) 978-0-9838793-7-4

Drawings from *Prisoner of War: Six years in Hanoi* by John M. McGrath, LCDR U.S. Navy, Copyright © 1975 U.S. Naval Institute, Annapolis, Maryland. Reprinted by Permission of Naval Institute Press

Cover design: A Better Buzz Brand Design
Interior Art and Layout Design: James Armstrong
Editor: Anne Alexander

Trade distribution is provided by the Greenleaf Book Group. To purchase this book for trade distribution, go to FreedomStarMedia.com/Media.

Media representation is provided by Smith Publicity Inc. For media requests and interviews, go to FreedomStarMedia.com/Media.

Publisher's Cataloging-in-Publication data

>Names: Ellis, Lee, 1943-, author.
>Title: Engage with honor : building a culture of courageous accountability / Lee Ellis.
>Description: Includes bibliographical references and index. | Cumming, Georgia: FreedomStar Media, 2016.
>Identifiers: ISBN 978-0- 9838793-7- 4 (Hardcover) | ISBN 978-0- 9838793-8- 1 (ebook) | LCCN 2016944122
>Subjects: LCSH Leadership. | Success in Business. | Organizational change. | Organizational effectiveness. | Character. | Courage. | BISAC BUSINESS & ECONOMICS / Leadership | BUSINESS & ECONOMICS / Management. | BUSINESS & ECONOMICS / Workplace Culture.
>Classification: LCC HD57.7 .E419 2016 | DDC 658.4/092--dc23

Special Sales
FreedomStar Media resources are available at special discounts for bulk purchases for sale promotions or premiums. Special editions, including personalized covers or bookplate inscriptions, excerpts of existing books, and corporate imprints, can be created in large quantities for special needs. For more information, please contact us at Contact@FreedomStarMedia.com.

 Printed in the USA

FreedomStar Media·   16 17 18 19 20 – 10 9 8 7 6 5 4 3 2
1st Printing

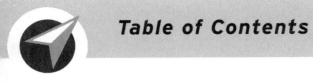

Table of Contents

ENGAGE WITH HONOR

Foreword

I CAN'T THINK OF MANY individuals who can write more authentically about honor as it relates to leadership and engagement than Lee Ellis. As an American POW, he survived 1,955 days of captivity in North Vietnam, where he saw fellow POW leaders—including Sen. John McCain—courageously uphold their honor and integrity in the toughest conditions.

I've had the pleasure of working with Lee in his civilian life as a leadership consultant and have admired the way he uses those experiences to help executives develop their own leadership models. He and I share a passion for doing business the honorable way and for developing leaders who will embody the character and the values that will help lead their organizations with the highest integrity.

Lee shared the foundation of his leadership philosophy in his first book, *Leading with Honor*. In this new book, Lee expands the concept of honor in leadership and introduces the model to build a culture of Courageous Accountability, drawing on some of his POW experiences as examples.

In today's fast-changing environment, marked by techno-logical changes happening at warp speed, global competition and fluid business models, leaders are challenged with mak-ing difficult choices, often in uncharted territory. Leaders at all levels of experience will benefit from Lee's leadership compass and Courageous Accountability Model as they navigate their organizations and teams on the right path to success.

Ralph de la Vega,
Vice Chairman of AT&T Inc. and
CEO of AT&T Business Solutions
and AT&T International,
Author of *Obstacles Welcome:*
Turn Adversity to Advantage in
Business and Life

Introduction

HAVE YOU THOUGHT about the word *honor* and reflected on what it means? How can one word be so powerful and yet so abstract? It's both a noun and a verb. Think about it. We give VIPs a place of honor to sit, and then they might stand to speak and say, "It's an honor to have the opportunity to address you." We like to honor our veterans, and honorable people work hard to honor their commitments.

Though there are many nuances of this word, they all seem to connote something elevated, special, and right. It brings to mind truth, fidelity, and many aspects of what we hold high—some essence that we all can aspire to attain and give. In addition for our purposes here, we are looking at honor as an essential ingredient of trust and the binding agent in any long-lasting recipe for success. Fortunately, it has been a consistent thread throughout my entire life.

From the earliest days of my childhood, the charge to honor God, parents and our community set the standard for the way we were expected to live. Honor was firmly imbedded in the Alma Mater of my high school and college and modeled throughout my four years of military training in Air Force ROTC. We wanted to honor our country, our flag, those appointed over us, and the uniform we wore.

Three days after graduating from the University of Georgia, I was commissioned and entered flight school. Less than two years later I began flying combat missions in Southeast Asia, mainly over North Vietnam. On my 53rd mission I was shot down and captured. During the next five and a half years as a POW, there were many days when my commitment to honor my country and my fellowmen in the camps was the primary motivator that enabled me to live up to the Military Code of Conduct,[1] and fulfill our mission, vision, and values, all summarized in three words—Return with Honor.

After the war I returned to flying and had a wonderful military career. It was an honor to serve. For the last eighteen years I've been a leadership consultant, coach, author, and speaker. What an honor and a joy it has been to help leaders gain freedom to lead higher.

In the last four years I've turned much of my focus to the idea of honor. This word that has been a gentle and constant refrain from the beginning has become the core of my message. The previous book was to help people lead with honor; here the intent is to go deeper and to share ideas on how to engage with honor by focusing on its guardian companion—accountability. Let's take a quick overview of the book.

THE STRUGGLE FOR HONOR

It seems that citizens of the entire civilized world are crying out, "Where is the honor?" Why are so many unwilling to keep their commitments? Why do we see so many shamelessly put their own self-interests above their constituents, their customers, their organizations, their teammates? Where are those who are willing to make sacrifices to keep their word and honor their commitments?

I am reminded of the dramatic line from the movie *Apollo 13* that so many of that era recall and still use to indicate something is not right—"Houston, we have problem." But it isn't just a spaceship orbiting around the earth; it's our entire earth orbiting around the sun—we have a planetary problem with honor.

It should be no great surprise that we are in this predicament. We human beings have struggled with this from the beginning of time—it's in our DNA. We have free will and with that comes the opportunity to choose to be not only self-focused enough to survive, but also to be selfish to the point of violating others' trust and our commitments in order to get what we want.

When wisdom, humility, and good judgment prevail, we usually make good choices and live honorably. But even with a commitment to ethical and moral values and strong self-discipline, we can still get off track in our integrity and honor—no one is perfect.

ACCOUNTABILITY – THE GUARDIAN COMPANION OF HONOR

The reality is that accountability and consequences are part of the natural laws of nature. The bad choice of leaping off a tall building challenges the law of gravity and gravity has no friends or enemies; it treats everyone the same. Consider the longstanding nature of the following expressions that likely exist in every culture in the world. Generally, they are pointing out the built-in tendency for natural accountability.

- ▶ You reap what you sow.
- ▶ If you play with fire you get burned.
- ▶ Time will tell.
- ▶ What goes around comes around.
- ▶ Sooner or later the other shoe will fall.

There does seem to be a natural law here that accountability eventually comes. If you have sown good deeds and words, the consequences will be rewarding, while sowing in a negative or unhealthy manner will result in problems. Wise people welcome the guardrails that accountability provides to keep them on track and avoid going over the cliff.

It seems reasonable and helpful to refer to accountability as the guardian companion of honor. This guardrail won't solve all the problems. Reckless choices and behaviors can still cause career and life "derailments," but it seems like a good place to start.

And speaking of starting, the best place to begin this journey of honor and accountability is with ourselves. Of course we'd like to get everyone else to "straighten up and act right," but for the most part, we have to begin with ourselves and the influence we have over others in our day-to-day workplace and home.

The ultimate goal of this book is to help you engage with honor. The immediate objective is to provide some specific steps that you can use to become more effective in every aspect of honor and accountability. The context is primarily focused on work situations, but the ideas and skills will apply to any setting—even at home. In fact, that's a good place to practice many of the skills and changes needed for our personal and leadership development.

ENGAGE WITH THE
COURAGEOUS ACCOUNTABILITY MODEL™

If you think this book is going to tell you how to beat up on all those people who don't come through, you'll be disappointed. Confronting those who don't keep their commitments is covered—but those situations are going to be minimized. Your time is much better spent on helping people be successful. In fact, as you read through the chapters (and the accountability books referenced in the endnotes) you'll see that most leadership experts and authors believe that 90 percent or more of us want to be successful—and can be—with good leadership. Hence, the focus is on helping you grow as a leader so you can facilitate the success of your followers. If you adopt a positive mindset about accountability and follow this model, you are going to be spending much more time celebrating than confronting.

> ▶ **Section 1 -** "The Struggle for Honor" (Chapters 1-3) makes the case for living and leading with honor and employing courageous accountability to help in that effort.

> ▶ **Section 2 -** "The Courageous Accountability Model" (Chapters 4-10) begins with the core of the model: Character, Courage, and Commitment. It all starts with the leader's accountability to those three C's—linked with effective Communications.

The model then progresses logically through the steps of Clarify, Connect, Collaborate and Closeout (Celebrate or Confront). We've tried to make this a very "how to" oriented book. We've also included several other models that we use to help leaders and teams grow to a higher level of performance. Following the format of *Leading with Honor*, each chapter opens with a story from the POW camps and concludes with "Mission Prep" coaching questions and a Foot Stomper that summarizes the highlights of the chapter.

There are several recurring themes throughout, and the strongest one is the idea that it takes a great deal of courage to lead and engage with honor. It's a daily struggle. I invite you to join me in this battle as we engage with honor—not only for ourselves, but for the next generation that will soon replace us.

Development of leaders is a key theme. Boomers are retiring quickly, Gen Xers are in short supply, and Millennials are already taking our place. They have grown up in a very different world from most of us. Our legacy is to pass the torch of honor and accountability. If we set the example and engage them courageously, we can do it.

Thank you for taking this challenge. I look forward to hearing from you as you engage with honor and build a culture of courageous accountability.

Lee Ellis

ENDNOTES

1   See Appendix C for Military Code of Conduct or at http://www.au.af.mil/au/awc/awcgate/readings/code_of_conduct.htm

SECTION ONE:

 The Struggle for Honor

THERE IS A PART OF OUR NATURE that wants life to be easy. There is nothing wrong with that—except most of the time it's just not that way. Success usually comes at a price. In *The Return of the King* there is a great line, "There is no glory without suffering." In the movie *Unbroken* as Louis Zamperini was departing to go to Berlin to run in the 1936 Olympics, his older brother Pete looked him in the eye and said, "Louis. A moment of pain is worth a lifetime of glory."[1]

To be the person you want to be, you must commit to a struggle. Honor cannot be inherited or assumed; it must be fought for on a daily basis. I learned that early in life while serving and surviving in the crucible of Vietnam POW camps.

The letter below is an unedited excerpt from a three-page letter I wrote to my parents on March 12, 1973, two days before our release. My purpose was to help them understand a son they had not seen in almost six years. After spending 1,955 days there in captivity and knowing I would soon be free, you can see that my main goal was to continue a struggle—the one that I had already begun—to engage with honor.

12 March 1973

Dear Family,

I am hopeful that the next three days will bring silver wings to bear me back to the land of milk and honey, to freedom and a wonderful reunion with you. For you, I know these many years have been very difficult and I regret that you have had to suffer so much. We have a saying here, "It's harder on them than on us," because for you there has been uncertainty and many ups and downs. We have had faith and confidence in your welfare, but for you our situation was mostly unknown.

For me, the years have passed rather rapidly and yet it seems that the first 23 years of my life were a dream, or perhaps the experiences of a person whom I once knew. This has become a way of life and the world in which you have lived was a faraway thing. Yet at no time have I ever given up my faith in God, my family, my country and those things for which our heritage has always stood.

My mental health has fared quite well also, I think. Of course my only measure is my memory and a comparison with those in this closed society. I have matured and I think my judgment is better. I have learned more about responsibility and I think you will find me more industrious. I have gained self-confidence and a deep sense of pride. By that I mean that if I do a job I want to do the best job possible, for to do less would bring dishonor upon myself, and those who believe in me would be disappointed. I feel that I have learned a great deal about human nature from myself and those with whom I have lived so intimately these past years. I have learned patience and understanding and to try to do those things which should be done when the opportunity arises.

To imply that I've perfected these virtues would be far from the truth for I have not, nor shall I ever. But here lies the essence of my philosophy. To constantly work to improve in these areas and to always be correcting back to the course which I have charted for my life. I believe that happiness in life comes from achievement; not just materialistic achievement, but more specifically in the small victories gained from day-to-day in man's struggle to be the type of person that he thinks he should be.

This achievement not only brings honor to the man and his family, but more important it glorifies God. The last line of the poem which my roommate has just written sums up these ideas quite well." More majestic monuments than men who live their faith cannot be found."

I hope that I have not sounded too egotistical nor philosophized too much, but I wanted to paint a picture of myself. Granted, it has been from my own eyes, so you could know what to expect ...

All my love,
Lee

As we move into the three chapters of Section 1, we'll look at the costs of dis-honor, the battle for honor, and the role of accountability in helping us preserve honor and achieve true success. I trust that you will see the need for honor, the way forward, and the rewards of engaging with honor and its guardian companion, courageous accountability.

ENDNOTES

1   http://www.wingclips.com/movie-clips/unbroken/moment-of-pain

ONE:

Critical Failures in Honor

"To know what is right and not do it is the worst cowardice."

~ Confucius

THE F-4 PHANTOM was powerful, supersonic and highly reliable.[1] But when ours was hit over enemy territory, it folded like a wounded duck on opening day. Fortunately, the ejection system worked perfectly. Unfortunately, it launched me from the protected womb of the cockpit into my worst personal and professional nightmare—a nylon letdown into the hands of the gunners below. We were some sixty miles into enemy territory—there was no way to evade. I was captured immediately, as was my partner whom I would not see again for ten days.

Hands tied, blindfolded and with a rope around my neck, I was pulled along like a reluctant hound, as we wound our way through bamboo hamlets toward the nearest "truck park" on the Ho Chi Minh Trail. Externally I had remained calm, the result of my training and default discipline. But as the shock wore off and the reality of my situation sank in, I fought an internal battle with fear. On one hand, their militia displayed a degree of order and control, which calmed me. On the other hand, I was an American pilot taken prisoner in an area we had been bombing for more than two years.

Several times when the locals discovered I was passing through, they came after me with a vengeance. I survived only because of the honorable leadership of the Vietnamese sergeant in charge of my detail. He did his duty, protecting me and making sure I was delivered safely to the collection prison farther north, near the provincial town of Vinh.

As we got closer to Hanoi, the anxiety I felt was likely similar to what soldiers have felt throughout the ages as they closed into battle. I had fears, but I would lean in and do my best. My new battle would be to live up to my responsibilities as outlined in the Code of Conduct[2] for prisoners of war. I knew I would be held accountable by others, but first and most importantly, I was accountable to myself. I did not want to fail in keeping my commitments—someday I wanted to return with honor.

On the last leg of this agonizing journey north, I joined up with my aircraft commander and fellow pilot, Capt. Ken Fisher, as well as two other POWs. We were bound and then tied to the side rails of a military truck. As we hit partially repaired bomb craters and mud holes, we repeatedly bounced high in the air and then slammed down on the truck floor for 8-10 hours each night. One of the two new guys was Lt. Col. Minter,[3] who would be our senior officer—at least for a short while.

The four of us who had made that journey north together ended up in a small six and a half foot by seven-foot cell at Hỏa Lò (the infamous Hanoi Hilton). It soon became clear that our senior ranking officer (SRO) did not share the same values and perspectives on our country's role in the war. Though a gung-ho leader prior to his shoot down, he now freely provided military-related information to the enemy and defended their positions on the war. It was both angering and agonizing to see my leader failing in his duties.

Hỏa Lò (Hanoi Hilton)

Fortunately, I was not the only one deeply troubled by our senior officer's behavior. While Minter was away at a "quiz" one day, Capt. Fisher, our second ranking officer, shared his concerns about Minter's actions. He asked Lt. Warner (our other cellmate) and me if we would support him if he removed our senior ranking officer (SRO) from command and took over our cell. That was a huge step. In essence we would mutiny, and we had no idea how it would play out. But clearly something needed to be done, so we agreed that it would be the best course of action under the circumstances; we would give Capt. Fisher[4] our full allegiance.

The tension in our cell escalated when Minter returned and Fisher confronted him. Minter seemed a little surprised, but did not become overly hostile, explaining that because this was not a declared war, the Code of Conduct did not apply, and basically, it was every man for himself. Even as a fresh twenty-four-year-old lieutenant, I knew better and could not have imagined anyone responding this way. He was rationalizing to the point of being irrational. Sure, our situation had changed by the nature of our capture, but as military members, our responsibilities and accountability were even more crucial now than before.

Minter's response was beyond disappointing. Listening to him defend his abandonment of duty, I saw firsthand how a leader's character could crumble when faced with a difficult choice to do the right thing to fulfill his duty—especially when the consequences might be painful. It appeared that Minter decided his self-interest mattered more than his professional commitments. Or, to put it another way, he was willing to abandon his honor to better his situation in the moment.

In contrast, Captain Fisher turned out to be the exact opposite kind of leader. He endured torture and suffering to do his duty and remain faithful to our cause. As my SRO for nearly three years, he modeled honor and courage—inspiring me to grow stronger and helping me to become the person I am today.[5]

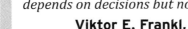

> *"In the concentration camps, for example, in this living laboratory and on this testing ground, we watched and witnessed some of our comrades behave like swine while others behaved like saints. Man has both potentialities within himself; which one is actualized depends on decisions but not on conditions."*
> **Viktor E. Frankl,**
> Psychiatrist, WWII Holocaust Survivor, and Author of *Man's Search for Meaning*

DIS-HONORABLE* BEHAVIOR
RUNS DEEP IN OUR DNA

Neglecting one's duty and pursuing selfish choices is part of the human condition; it's been that way since the beginning of time. Consider the example of David, the shepherd boy who slew the giant Goliath and later became king. You probably know the story of this revered leader and historical figure, but it's worth reviewing as we engage the subject of honor and accountability.

From his early youth David was known for his courage and his commitment to honor God. As a young shepherd he killed bears with his bare hands. As an adult, he was the most famous and celebrated warrior in the history of Israel. When Saul died in battle, David became a beloved and successful king.

And then one spring when kings normally go off to war, he stayed home. That's when his downfall began—on a warm day when he looked down from his roof and saw Bathsheba bathing. She happened to be the wife of one of his soldiers. David sent for her and had his way. When she became pregnant, David hatched a simple scheme to conceal his problem and protect Bathsheba from scandal—he would bring Bathsheba's husband, Uriah, back from the war for a few days of R&R with his wife.

But Uriah—being a man of great loyalty to his fellow soldiers—refused to go home to Bathsheba. Instead, he slept at the palace with the servants. David's cover-up ploy was foiled, so his deception intensified. He sent Uriah back to the battle with orders to Joab, his general, to make sure that Uriah was at the front of the attack. Then he was to pull back and let him be killed. It worked. Then David brought Bathsheba to the palace as his wife.

---

* We have intentionally shown the word *dishonor* as "dis-honor" to emphasize the prefix associated with honor in this instance (the "Dis" prefix meaning "apart," "asunder," "away," "utterly," or having a privative, negative, or reversing force).

Later, the prophet Nathan confronted David in an amazing exchange that brought repentance. David was forgiven, but the consequences of his actions were disastrous. The child died and David's family was plagued with dysfunction—including incest, rape, murder, rebellion, and the death of his son, Absalom. David lost the trust and confidence of his people, and his life and leadership were never the same.

David had been "a man after God's own heart," yet he had acted as though he could take what he wanted without consequences. When he feared his deeds would be exposed, he used his power to cover up, protect his image, and avoid the negative consequences. But accountability eventually came.

Isn't it amazing how this story parallels so much of what we see today? It's common to hear about a leader who commits a crime—or some ethical violation—and then weaves an intricate cover-up. And when that begins to unravel, we hear outright denials, and then the blame game escalates—along with more excuses, justifications, and rationalizations. Typically, the whistle-blowers are demonized. And sometimes the guilty try to destroy the reputation of their accusers, or use their power to bury them figuratively—and sometimes literally. These are the high profile ones (like David) we hear so much about, but we all carry this same mutated gene that drives our egos to try to take whatever we want, without really considering what's ultimately at stake. When honor fails, we all lose; when honor fails and there is a lack of accountability, the loss undermines the culture and the structure of the organization.

FAILURES IN INDUSTRY

In recent years, key players in the auto industry have stumbled, failing to do the honorable thing. At least three automakers have dominated the news by their persistent denial of alleged problems in some of their vehicles.

In these cases, they disavowed any culpability for years until they were confronted with evidence by state and federal authorities. Only then did they finally come clean—at least the leaders did—but the aftermath affected millions of their shareholders, employees, and customers.

FAILURES IN GOVERNMENT

Our citizens are dismayed by the performance of our government and its agencies. Politics aside, let's look at the evidence. Only 17 percent of the country has a favorable impression of Congress, yet no one seems to be able to hold them accountable. Regardless of which party is in power, the national debt grows at an ever-increasing rate to the point that the curve looks like a hockey stick.

The EPA has been under fire for their inability to deal with dis-honorable behavior. In one case it was a top-level employee accused of viewing porn several hours a day while at work. Even though investigators found 7,000 pornographic files on his computer and even caught him watching porn, he remained on the payroll.[6] In another situation, leaders involved in ongoing sexual harassment—for more than ten years—were allowed to retire with full pensions. They were not held accountable.[7]

The most persistent failure from a government agency (at least according to the news) seems to be the VA (Veterans Administration). Over the past several years, repeatedly there has been a new horror story of mismanagement, deception, duplicity and most troubling of all—a lack of accountability.

There are similar stories from the alphabet soup of agencies that spend our hard-earned money. Consider the following examples:

- ▶ GSA (General Services Administration) indulged in Las Vegas at our expense.
- ▶ IRS has been under fire for unethical practices.[8]
- ▶ GAO (Government Accounting Office) has investigated CMS (Center for Medicaid and Medicare Services), which is a part of the Dept. of HHS (Health and Human Services). They've found significant problems with oversight of monies provided by CMS to the states for the implementation of state health care exchanges. Basically, millions of dollars are not accounted for by the state or the federal government.[9] Did it just disappear? No one seems to know. Where is the honor? Where is the accountability?
- ▶ The DOE (Department of Energy) blew $500 million on Solyndra, a company on the verge of going broke— as well as millions more in other "green" energy companies that went under. The *Washington Post* did extensive research and reporting on the "Solyndra Scandal" and concluded that government documents showed that "Obama's green-technology program was infused with politics at every level."[10]

The question that seems to have normal working people scratching their heads is, "Can anybody in the government be fired for ethical and performance failures?" Actually, there's been a sick joke going around for quite a while now—"A civil service employee is much more likely to die of a heart attack at work than to be fired." Sad, but probably true. Where is the accountability? Where is the honor?

As you would expect, the DOD (Department of Defense) seems to have done a better job of firing people for ethical violations than the other departments. Still, it is concerning that a spate of dis-honorable and illegal behaviors by generals and admirals is undermining the "good order and discipline" of the armed services. For example: an admiral fired for gambling with fake poker chips, generals and admirals disciplined for sexual harassment, assault, alcohol abuse, and improper use of government assets for personal benefit.[11] And then there is General Petraeus. One can only conclude that success and power skewed his ethical compass, and the honor of one of our true heroes was shattered. What happened to his honor code?

FAILURES IN FINANCIAL SERVICES

Enron was a fast-rising flash in the pan. Arthur Andersen was old, established, and respected. Together, they were tossed into the pile of fallen icons—gone forevermore, because they lost sight of honor. Then in 2008 we learned that many banks and their Wall Street hucksters were selling bundles of loans that looked good on the outside, but on the inside they were rank with risk. The Ponzi scheme worked for a while, but eventually someone was left holding the bag—the American taxpayer. Do you recall TARP? You should. It cost you $475 Billion—that's with a B.[12]

FAILURES IN EDUCATION

You would think that educators—those responsible for developing our youth—would be above these self-centered, take-care-of-myself behaviors. But not so. The former Chicago Public Schools chief pled guilty to steering "more than $23 million in no-bid contracts from the school system to her previous employers in exchange for kickbacks that would have made her millions of dollars."[13]

In the Atlanta public schools, thirty-five educators and administrators were convicted of racketeering when they conspired to change students' answers on standardized tests in order for the students to get higher scores. The goal was to protect the educators from the consequences of not meeting standards set by the No Child Left Behind Act. The kids were left even further behind as the teachers scrambled to the trough to feed their own needs. Where was the honor? Eventually, there was accountability and the consequences came too.

At a small local high school in North Georgia, thirty-five students were accused of cheating in their online AP US History course—after they were caught sharing answers through their Google accounts. The school superintendent said, "Most students confessed to cheating and know what they did was wrong."[14] Don't you wonder why they did something they knew was wrong? I wonder to what degree they might have been affected by the general loss of honor in our society, and how that might have been expedited by dis-honorable behaviors by high profile leaders and famous performers who seem to get away with a lot—with a wink and a nod.

FAILURES IN HONOR

Honor suffers from Main Street to Pennsylvania Avenue. The story above about top high school students cheating reminds us that honor issues are not just revealed in folks who are "out there." Character and ethical failures are in our neighborhoods, in our homes, and even in us—if we fail to be "on guard." Reflect with me.

An Illinois cop embezzled funds from youth organizations

to pay off his mortgage and to pay for adult websites. Rather than face the music, he committed suicide—making it look like he was a murder victim. In my immediate region, I'm aware of an HR manager in a Christian ministry who embezzled money from the funds set aside for medical payments. Two nearby Chamber of Commerce managers—as well as bookkeepers and employees in several other local county offices—have gone to jail for embezzlement. In every case these were solid citizens from good families.

Last year I was in San Antonio to speak for a client's event. When I checked into the hotel, the headlines of the local paper proclaimed: "Lawyer pleads guilty to bribing state court judge."[15] That was an eye opener, but it didn't stop there. In the first section of the paper I counted stories of twelve different ethical violations. While writing this chapter, the campus pastor at a large local church resigned, confessing years of adultery, leaving a disappointed congregation and more importantly a shattered life for his wife and three children.

In David's time they wanted kings. Today in our country, we have presidents, governors and mayors—but not much else has changed. If we assume that our top public servants' track record of honor is replicated in the culture, we can estimate the magnitude of the problem. In my lifetime I've seen President Nixon resign in the face of impeachment for Watergate and its cover-up. President Clinton was impeached by the House of Representatives for perjury and obstruction of justice.[16] There have been apparent ethical scandals in several of the other administrations from both political parties.

Does it mean anything that one state has three governors that have gone to prison? The long list of mayors of large cities that have been locked up for dis-honorable service is telling about the human condition.[17] (Take a look at the link in this endnote.)

We see how easy it is not only for regular people like our next door neighbors—but also the nation's highest, most powerful leaders—to slide into arrogant, selfish assumptions, thinking they are above the law and choosing to do what is right in their own eyes. The lesson is clear. We are all cut from the same cloth. Without clear standards and intentional accountability, we can lose our true north and thus, our honor. Without a consistent commitment to character, our sense of duty, responsibility, accountability, and honor fades away.

"Without honor a society can slip into chaos and even tyranny."
Lee Ellis

We must take a stand for honor. As the POWs took a stand to return with honor, we must each take a stand to engage with honor—both within ourselves and with our teams. In the next chapter, we'll look at what that will require. But before we go further, take time now to reflect on your perspectives regarding honor, using the Mission Prep and Foot Stomper features below.

MISSION PREP

1. Do you agree that we are all capable of dis-honorable behavior?
2. Have you ever done something dis-honorable? How did it turn out? What would you do differently now?
3. What do you think causes good people to do dis-honorable deeds?
4. How do you personally guard against dis-honorable behavior?
5. How can you influence our younger generations to live and lead with honor?

Watch Lee's Coaching Clip on this chapter.
Go to EngageWithHonor.com

FOOT STOMPER[18]

Honor is not automatic—it cannot be assumed. The strongest and most courageous leaders in history have fallen short. Everyday people like you and me are lying, stealing, cheating, and embezzling. You and I can win this battle if we truly believe that honor matters—and we are diligent to hold ourselves accountable. Our example will influence others—leadership always makes a difference.

ENDNOTES

1 See a photo of the phantom at Appendix A.
2 See Appendix C for Code of Conduct or at http://www.au.af.mil/au/awc/awcgate/readings/code_of_conduct.htm
3 Not his real name.
4 http://veterantributes.org/TributeDetail.php?recordID=1380
5 On the upside, Capt. Fisher was our new senior ranking officer (SRO) and over the next two plus years, his wise and courageous leadership inspired me and others to even higher levels of commitment and resistance. Like the other great leaders in that crucible, he went first into the torture and deprivation, courageously setting the example for others. You can read more in my previous book *Leading with Honor: Leadership Lessons from the Hanoi Hilton*.
6 CBS This Morning, March 2, 2015 http://www.cbsnews.com/news/civil-servant-protection-system-could-keep-problematic-government-employees-from-being-fired/
7 http://federalnewsradio.com/workforce/2015/07/epa-ignored-sexual-harassment-decade-whistleblowers-claim/
8 http://www.washingtontimes.com/news/2016/apr/14/federal-judge-irs-untrustworthy-tea-party-case/
9 http://www.gao.gov/assets/680/672565.pdf
10 https://www.washingtonpost.com/politics/specialreports/solyndra-scandal/
11 https://www.washingtonpost.com/world/national-security/military-brass-behaving-badly-files-detail-a-spate-of-misconduct-dogging-armed-forces/2014/01/26/4d06c770-843d-11e3-bbe5-6a2a3141e3a9_story.html
12 http://www.investopedia.com/terms/t/troubled-asset-relief-program-tarp.asp
13 http://www.usatoday.com/story/news/2015/10/08/former-chicago-public-schools-ceo-indicted/73595890/#
14 Megan Studdard and Mat Payne, "Rabun County High School: Students knew they were wrong." May 7, 2015, ©the claytontribune.com.
15 http://www.mysanantonio.com/news/local/article/San-Antonio-lawyer-bribed-Bexar-judge-5323573.php
16 http://www.washingtonpost.com/wp-srv/national/longterm/watergate/articles/080974-3.htm, http://www.history.com/this-day-in-history/president-clinton-impeached, https://en.wikipedia.org/wiki/Clinton_v._Jones
17 http://www.citymayors.com/politics/us-corrupt-mayors.html
18 In flight training and many military training programs, the instructors will tell the students that "If I stomp my foot on a topic, you had better know it because it's very important and likely to be on the exam." Hence, the term Foot Stomper is widely used to underscore important points, and that's the way we'll use the term to underscore the key points of each chapter.

TWO:

Battling for Honor and Accountability

*"I have had more trouble with myself than
with any other man I have ever met."*[1]

~ Dwight Lyman Moody

WHEN WE MOVED AWAY from our deposed SRO, Lt. Col. Minter, he continued his wayward path and expanded his negative influence. In a clever move, our captors put him with another senior officer who had similar views. Soon a third insecure senior joined them and came under the spell of the two ringleaders. A year or so later, the V added several recently captured junior officers to this group. The new guys didn't know much about the camp situation—their cell was all they knew, so for a while they were heavily influenced by the three senior reprobates.

Fortunately, the camp situation changed two years later when the V responded to a Special Operations raid on the Son Tay camp, where 53 of us had lived for two years (but vacated four months prior to the raid). Fearing another raid, the V quickly moved almost all POWs in North Vietnam back to the heart of the capital to Hỏa Lò prison (the Hanoi Hilton) where

we occupied a section formerly inhabited by Vietnamese prisoners. To our amazement and delight, there were some 330
POWs in one location. With excellent, covert communications
we came together in a way never before experienced in the
camps. Our leaders named our new digs "Camp Unity." And
they designated our war-weary but still ornery group as a formal military unit, the 4th Allied POW Wing.

As soon as we were settled in and had identified who
was in camp, the senior staff sent a message to the reprobate
leaders and their followers, stating that they must "repent" and
follow the Code of Conduct. If they chose to make that commitment, they would be forgiven and accepted back into our
POW organization and community. If not, they would face serious consequences—alienation from the group and court martial proceedings after the war. Within a few weeks, all but two
(Minter and one other senior officer from the original three)
pledged their allegiance, agreeing to follow the rules. Their
attitudes and behaviors fell in line, and they remained in good
standing with our team. They corrected back on course and
came home with honor. Unfortunately, the other two remained
outcasts—barred from command authority and denied access
to sensitive camp information, with formal consequences to
come after repatriation. They were among the very few who
didn't return with honor.

Considering the suffering and sacrifices our senior leaders
had endured in their efforts to live by the code and fulfill their
duties, this positive approach of offering a fresh start seemed
almost counterintuitive. In fact, some in our group strongly disagreed with this grace policy, believing it to be too lenient. But
our leaders stuck to their decision. Their wisdom in showing
both strength and compassion set an example for the rest of us,

one that continues to inform my understanding of honor and accountability.

A CULTURE OF HONOR

Over the years since our return, I've had many people say, "I couldn't have done what you guys did." Others ask, "How did you guys do it? How were you able to resist the enemy, even when you knew they had the power to make you submit?" Like battling cancer and other unique life challenges, ours is hard to explain to the person who hasn't walked through the experience. Let me share my perspective.

In retrospect, most of the POWs grew up in the '30s, '40s, and '50s, so we were part of the "traditional" generation. Expectations for work and responsibility were taught and accountability was very important. Children were generally taught to honor God and their parents and to respect their elders, especially their teachers. One could argue that in that era honor played a more important role than in more recent generations.

Moreover, those of us who entered in military service experienced a strong and consistent message about responsibility and personal accountability that began in the earliest days of basic training. Such indoctrination was a key part of our culture—what the military calls "good order and discipline"— and clearly it gave us a common standard of expectations for ourselves and others. This "no excuse, sir" attitude toward responsibility and accountability equipped both the individual and the organization with the mindset and backbone to stand strong in the face of temptation and adversity.

With this foundation, even when thrown in the crucible of a POW camp, leaders and followers alike knew what was expected—to choose honor and do your duty to the best of your ability. For everyone (and especially our leaders) that meant enduring the pain and horrors of torture and isolation in order to fulfill their commitments. As they clearly demonstrated, the honorable way often means making hard choices that require sacrifice, even suffering in the moment. As a follower, hard choices were much easier when you saw your leaders setting the example.

For me personally, the example of my parents was also important. Life was hard, but they leaned into the pain to do the right thing. Likewise the responsibilities of growing up on a farm in the '50s, and the grind of five years of football practice played a key role in my makeup. But beyond those early influences, it was the military training and the example of my POW leaders and teammates that motivated me to choose honor. I wanted to live up to their standards and expectations and match their level of commitment.

In the context of living honorably, there was another quality that was essential—accountability. The guardian companion of honor was the idea of personal accountability—at home and at school. And then later, the importance of accountability was reinforced in my military life. Those in authority were preparing me for the future by making sure that I understood that I was responsible for my actions. And all along the way, it was made very clear that there would definitely be consequences affecting me (and others) if I didn't come through. That critical preparation paid off when facing temptations and difficult times.

The fears about POW camps that people imagine were definitely there. Just hearing the jailer's keys rattling at odd hours would cause my stomach to swirl and sink. But I was inspired and supported by a culture of honorable leadership and personal accountability. As a young lieutenant, without the courageous examples of senior leaders like Fisher, Risner, Denton, Stockdale, Day and so many more, making hard choices to stay on the path of honor would have been much more difficult for me. It's hard to imagine what it would have been like without them.

THE BATTLE FOR HONOR

The sad stories of lost honor in Chapter 1 aren't just for information—undoubtedly, you've already noticed this growing problem. The stories were intended to highlight the magnitude of the problem in today's culture, and even more to remind us that getting off course can happen to anyone, and that sooner or later there is a cost—consequences will come. Most importantly, I hope those stories stirred you to respond—to engage in the battle for honor on all fronts. Obviously, we can't saddle up and go out and fix all "those people" that are off course. That would be like charging windmills.

At the same time, I hope that you haven't given up in this battle for honor. Some, perhaps many, have put their heads in the sand, rather than engage in the issues. Even more disheartening are those who with a wink and a nod ignore dis-honorable behaviors—especially if the guilty are associated with the same race, religion, political ideology, or favorite sports team.

This mindset of tribal loyalty is common to human nature, but when related to accountability it can be very dangerous, taking us away from truth and justice. When "winning at the expense of truth" takes over, the "the ends justify the means" mentality follows right behind. We experienced this firsthand with the communists. They told us that truth was "that which most benefitted the party." Therefore, torturing POWs to sign false confessions was completely justified in their minds.

If we care about our freedom and the ethics of our culture, we must be proactive in the battle for honor. I want to invite you to join me in engaging and promoting the idea of honor, along with its guardian companion, accountability. You and I know it's not only a worthy challenge, but it's also an essential responsibility of citizens. Honor and truth are crucial to our culture and survival as a free society.

Regardless of how negative the societal landscape appears, I'm convinced that there is an overwhelming silent majority that believes in honor and accountability. We need to be heard on this critical subject; we can make a difference.

But it has to start with one—and before we can be heard, we have to be seen, *walking* the talk. Each individual that chooses to engage with honor can be like the leaders in the POW camps; we can engage and take others with us into this battle. If you serve in any capacity as a leader, then you have the responsibility and privilege of showing the way for others. You can lead them to a higher level. I know you can and I'm here to help. Let's get started.

IT TAKES MORE THAN GOOD INTENTIONS

Even when we're able to identify the honorable path forward, it doesn't necessarily make it any easier. In fact, often just the opposite occurs—if you can't cut corners, then you must work harder; you must make tougher choices. We have to overcome our natural inclination for the path of least resistance. Knowledge, clear thinking, and good logic are important tools for helping us overcome our natural inertia, but the hill of honor is a steep climb.

Good intentions, rationally made, are helpful, but usually not sufficient. Just consider the hall of shame that we recounted in Chapter 1 and the many other examples we've witnessed in recent years. We've seen the fall of politicians and public servants, preachers and pro athletes, professionals and practitioners, pundits and promoters, patriots and priests. These people didn't just wake up one morning and say, "Hey, I think I'll cut some corners and be dis-honorable today."

Most of us have learned about good character values. We know the talk—it's the walk that gets tough. The Watergate conspirators provide great insights into human frailty when faced with temptations that match our points of ambitious self-interests. These were bright, well-educated, successful professionals. Yet they made very serious—almost unbelievable—errors in judgment. What happened to their character? White House counsel Jeb McGruder explained this problem quite well saying, *"Somewhere between my ambition and my ideals, I lost my ethical compass. I found myself on a path that had not been intended for me by my parents or my principles or by my own ethical instincts."* [2]

So how do we stay on course? How do we guard our character and protect our honor?

Dave Cantu, www.ToonForWriters.com

As trite as it sounds, we need both a carrot and a stick. The carrot comes from our deepest desires, our strongest sources of energy—the source of our purest motives. These deep desires include needs like: to be safe and secure, to use our talents, to provide and protect, to be known and understood, to be valued and cared for, to love and be loved, to have meaning and purpose, and to come through in our assignments and hear, "Well done." There are others, but you can see how these can energize us to press on through hardship and sacrifice to reach a higher level.

You can also see how the drive to succeed in meeting these strong desires might get distorted and cause us to cut corners. If we are looking for an easy way or a quick fix, any of us can lose sight of true north on our ethical compass. Navigating by our selfish desires and arrogant beliefs is a time-tested tactic for losing our way. That's where the stick of courageous accountability has to be in play—the awareness that someone is going to hold us accountable. As in the character failures in Chapter 1, we will have to answer for our choices, behaviors, and actions; eventually, we will have to give an account. This awareness of consequences plays a key role in keeping human nature on track, climbing higher to reach our lofty goals. And that's why accountability is essential for: (1) successful living, (2) leading with honor, and (3) excellence in performance and execution.

THE ENEMY IS US

By now I hope you are convinced that every person is capable of dis-honorable behavior—that includes you and me. Andrew Carnegie, the famous industrialist of the 19th century, put it this way: *"All honor's wounds are self-inflicted."* [3]

In a more down home way, the famous cartoon character philosopher, Pogo the possum, expressed our situation by saying, "*We have met the enemy and he is us.*"

CORRECTING BACK MUST BE A WAY OF LIFE

Certainly there are things in my life that I'm not proud of—decisions and behaviors that I wish I could replay and do differently. That's not possible for anyone, but we can learn from our mistakes. We can use them to correct back on track. Early recognition allows us to make small corrections—before we get far out of positon or way off course.

As an instructor pilot teaching students how to fly the wing position in formation, I emphasized how important it was to always be correcting back to proper position. Small corrections are easy to make, but when you drift significantly out of position, recovery can be a challenge for even experienced pilots. Likewise in navigation, you have a planned course and checkpoints along the way. All pilots get off course and off altitude—but they learn to recognize it quickly and correct back.

The earlier story of Minter's followers is an example of good men that were influenced by bad leaders and got a bit off course. When accountability came, they recognized their error, made a course correction, and were welcomed back into the fold.

In the pursuit of honor there is no easy day—human nature can be weak—and temptations never sleep. The challenge for leaders is that we have to set the example for others while simultaneously fighting to stay on course ourselves. That kind of vulnerability only comes through self-confidence that is anchored in character, courage, and commitment. Capt. Fisher had it; Minter did not.

"The truth of the matter is that you always know the right thing to do. The hard part is doing it."

H. Norman Schwarzkopf,
General USA, Commander of Forces in the Persian Gulf War

SET THE EXAMPLE

As a leader you have great influence, and thus your personal battle for honor is crucial. People are watching you. Once while sitting in with a group of senior HR managers in a Fortune 500 company, I listened to a discussion about a particular manager in the company whose behaviors were rude and bullying. Surprising everyone, the senior VP spoke up and shared the shocking comment, "I used to behave like that routinely." Immediately heads snapped around with looks of disbelief and even some comments like, "No way." But the courageous VP came back, "Oh yes, I did. That's how my first boss operated, and so I thought that's the way leaders behaved. Eventually, another boss saw what I was doing, got my attention, and then mentored me on the power of respecting others. I learned that I could be kind and firm and get much better results."

This example of the bullying leader isn't as extreme as you might think. But you may have experienced more of the opposite—the passive leader—the one who fears to properly use his authority to lead and manage with courageous accountability. Maybe you have some characteristics of one or both of these extremes. How can you correct back? We'll cover the "how to" in much more detail in the chapters ahead, but it all begins with you, the individual—and you, the leader. Have you clarified your core beliefs and what characterizes honorable behavior?

Without that clarity, how will you know when you are drifting off course? How can you avoid losing your way like those who might have had good intentions, but ended up as an example of how not to live?

Recognizing that this concept of honor is broad and may bring to mind an assortment of images, our company decided to clarify and codify the foundational principles of what most of us would consider honorable behavior. We published it in the fall of 2014 as the Honor Code and have shared it with our clients and social media tribe.[4] Consider your example of honor in keeping these basic commitments.

HONOR CODE

This Honor Code was created to inspire leaders seeking to live with character, courage, and competence. These behaviors are the foundational principles for living and leading with honor.

1
Tell the truth, even when it's difficult.
Avoid duplicity and deceitful behavior.

2
Treat others with dignity and respect.
Take the lead, and show value to others.

3
Keep your word and your commitments.
Ask for relief sooner than later if necessary.

4
Be ethical.
Operate within the laws of the land, the guidelines of your profession, and the policies of your employer.

5
Act responsibly; do your duty, and be accountable.
Own your mistakes, and work to do better in the future.

6
Be courageous.
Lean into the pain of your fears to do what you know is right, even when it feels unnatural or uncomfortable.

7
Live your values.
Be faithful to your spiritual core, your conscience, and your deepest intuitions.

As you can see, the Honor Code is very simple. It seems so obvious—yet we all know that it's difficult to live up to these standards.

That's why the idea of regularly correcting back to course is so important. You can also imagine how great your influence will be when you consistently choose to engage with honor by authentically striving to live out these seven principles.

We must never forget that values, behavior, and honor are "caught" much more than they're "taught." We must become the example we want to see in others, knowing that the power of our example far exceeds what we might imagine. Use it wisely— engage with honor and be authentic when you fall short.

ACCOUNTABILITY IS YOUR FRIEND

If you are intent on guarding your character and correcting back to course, you are heading in the right direction. But it will require more than good intentions. You will need accountability, the practical, day-to-day guardian companion of honor. Living and leading in the light of accountability isn't easy, and it's not for the faint of heart. It requires character, courage, and commitment—and leaders must go first. In the chapters ahead, you'll see how to make accountability your friend and how to lead with friendly accountability.

MISSION PREP

1. On a scale of 1-10, how important is it for you to live and lead with honor? What deep desire(s) anchor your commitment to honor?

2. Are you convinced that your assumptions and intentions will not be sufficient to keep you on course with honor?

3. What will be the impact of your genuine commitment to engage with honor?

4. Can you be vulnerable and authentic about your walk by leading others while at the same time correcting back to course yourself?

Watch Lee's Coaching Clip on this chapter.
Go to EngageWithHonor.com

FOOT STOMPER

 Honor is acquired by winning daily battles to overcome our ego and distorted self-interests. It can be "taught," but it's more likely "caught" from the example of those most influential in our lives—especially our leaders. Accountability requires a carrot and a stick; we need both to stay on course.

ENDNOTES

1   http://www.quotegarden.com/integrity.html
2   Jeb S. Magruder, *An American LIfe: One Man's Road to Watergate*, Atheneum, 1974.
3   http://www.brainyquote.com/quotes/keywords/honor_2.
    html#BTzjMmy4puQBZeCy.99
4   You can download a full page color copy of the Honor Code from our website at
    www.leadingwithhonor.com.

THREE:

Building a Culture of Accountability

"A bias for results means being accountable to oneself and holding others accountable."

~ Bill Wiersma[1]

AFTER MORE THAN THREE YEARS of incarceration without any attacks near Hanoi, there was a general feeling in the camps that our political leaders lacked the will to truly prosecute the war. As military men, we knew that we were expendable in the big picture, but at the same time you want your team to win. And personally, we all longed to go home. Capt. Ken Fisher had a daughter he hadn't seen in five years; Capt. Smitty Harris had a seven-year-old son he had never met; Smitty could only imagine what he looked like. I wanted to see my family, and like everyone I longed for freedom. But compared to the married guys, I could never feel sorry for myself. I hurt too much for them.

The spring of 1972 brought changes in the war. With the warmer weather and the dryer conditions, the communist north launched a conventional style widespread invasion into the south. The first week of May the US responded with a vengeance, striking the railroads and factories near Hanoi. From our sideline seats, the fireworks were like New Year's Eve and the Fourth of July Independence Day celebration all rolled into one—only on steroids. Bomb explosions shook the ground, anti-aircraft artillery clapped in the skies, surface to air missile (SAM) launches provided the hissing sounds of rockets, and the supersonic booms from our fighter buddies overhead all combined to give us a glorious symphony—the long awaited sounds of rolling thunder[2] on a clear day.

Inside the prison walls we were celebrating—a few risked cheering out loud—and the ambience was electrifying. Everyone was energized and hopeful. You see, we believed that we might never get out unless the communist leaders were personally threatened. The guards were obviously terrified; seeing the fear in their eyes added to our optimism. This could be the beginning of the end.

Hỏa Lò Unity Compound

After a few day of attacks—on Mother's Day to be exact—they loaded half the camp into trucks and headed for the Chinese border. We assumed this move was to have us stashed away like an insurance policy. In case the US invaded or inadvertently struck the prison, they would have prisoners as hostages for leverage in negotiations. There was no way to know if the move was a good sign or a bad one—but for sure life was going to be different.

Riding blindfolded and handcuffed in the back of a canvas-covered truck wasn't new—most of us had done that several times when changing camps in the past. But this was a seventeen-hour jaunt of bouncing over bombed out roads, with little food and water. In the stress of the humid heat (along with the rough ride), some men struggled physically to keep their primary body systems working.

By the time the sun came up, even the guards were exhausted. They began to drop their "guard" somewhat, letting us take off our blindfolds. Through the back opening we could see some beautifully manicured rice fields and farmers driving their water buffaloes, carrying on as though they had not been troubled by this war, nor the many wars that the Tonkinese had fought against the Chinese in this buffer border over the last thousand years. Toward noon we were climbing via what seemed like unending switchbacks into the rugged and beautiful karst-like mountains, so often seen in pictures of Southeast Asia.

Mercifully, we finally arrived at our destination. The trucks stopped at a remote compound and delivered our group of some 205 POWs to a mountain camp just three kilometers from the Chinese border. This outpost (we named it Dogpatch) consisted of a dozen or so primitive buildings perched on the side of small rocky hills that were too rough to farm.

Each building housed 15-20 prisoners. The interior and exterior walls were constructed with crude slabs of limestone rock, more than a foot thick, giving the aroma and aura of an abandoned mine shaft. The cells were dirty and apparently had not been occupied by humans for some time. Our first task was to expel the critters that had taken up residence—the guys in one building were greeted by a cobra.

With all respects to Tom Bodett, it wasn't easy to "sleep well" in this motel—and there was no light left on to welcome us. Dogpatch was my only camp experience that had no electricity. The barred openings for windows were high on the walls and tiny, allowing only a sliver of light even on the sunniest days. It was a dreadfully dark place. The only warmth of home came from the solace of our brotherhood. At least we were not alone.

In August as I was closing out my fifth year as a POW, actress Jane Fonda made a two week "peace" visit to the DRV, communist North Vietnam.[3] After touring the country she made several emotional anti-war propaganda tapes for our enemy—and at least one was focused specifically toward US military fighters, claiming that we were using illegal weapons and intentionally bombing hospitals, schools, and dikes. This was pure false propaganda; her claims were completely alien to our rules of engagement.[4] Showing no respect for our military, or for our laws about aiding and abetting our enemies, she openly and shamelessly encouraged us to discontinue our war efforts.

A few weeks after her visit to North Vietnam, "Hotshot" (one of the English-speaking junior officers) came by and began setting up a battery-powered tape recorder in the largest cell in our building. Curly, our SRO, asked him, "What are we supposed to do with this?"

"You need to bring all the prisoners in here to listen to a message from Jane Fonda," Hotshot replied.

Under his breath and out of earshot Curly said, "Yeah, right. The guys will be pumped about this! Just what we all wanted to hear this morning—Jane Fonda's propaganda sermon!"

This summons to hear her message prompted a leadership challenge within our band of brothers. When the tape started rolling and Fonda basically called us "criminals," cellmate Ox stood up and staunchly refused to listen anymore saying, "No way am I gonna to sit here and listen to this crap!"

Watching this scene unfold, Oso stepped in and took up Ox's case and made it clear that he would join him in refusing to sit in on Fonda's broadcast. As Oso's disgust escalated, so did his rant. Curly became frustrated and you could see the steam coming out of his ears as he barked, "I order you to stay in this room—both of you!" The two turned their back and walked out the door, returning to their individual cells.

Although Curly disagreed completely with Fonda, he chose this occasion to openly demonstrate to the V that he (as the SRO) had control of his men. Hence, he wanted everyone to obey his command to stay put until the tape was over.

The rest of us felt the same as the two guys (Ox and Oso) who walked out of the room, but we went along with Curly to support his leadership in front of the V. There were also some challenging historical dynamics that played into this particular situation.

For years we had fought daily mental, physical, and emotional battles with our enemy, resisting their efforts to "brainwash" us to agree with them. They referred to us as "creeminals" and used torture in an attempt to extract antiwar propaganda. So it was now grafted into our DNA to resist hearing more false propaganda. Curly, however, was adamant that these two had crossed the line. "Ox and Oso, you disregarded my order and you must be held accountable, because your insubordination set a bad example for your fellow soldiers."

Within a couple of days, he convened a three-man court martial and quickly found them guilty of insubordination. To his credit as a fair leader, Curly later told Ox and Oso privately that nothing would come of it, and it never did. But the public issue was that they had disobeyed and there had to be accountability. They made their point and Curly made his point.[5]

Under the circumstances I could relate to both sides. No doubt, Curly's action reminded us that accountability is important and that we needed to back our leaders. On the other hand, this unique situation showed me how important it is for leaders to engage by clarifying their true goals, seeking "wise counsel" and connecting with the hearts of their people—before holding them accountable, and especially when there are matters of strong principles at stake.

A LOVE-HATE ATTITUDE

Our society seems to be somewhat schizophrenic about accountability. We hear passionate complaints about the lack of accountability across the spectrum—from the government, politics, education, and business to finance, religion, and the media. At the same time, when it comes to being on the receiving end, accountability seems to have earned a bad image. In fact, some people told me I should avoid using the word in this book, because it is so negative and often equated with frustration and injustice, even punishment. So in one way we want accountability, generally. But in another way we fear and reject it, personally.

Often when we see such a love-hate relationship, there is some sort of paradox going on underneath. In leadership there is apparent paradox at every turn, and in fact this can be what makes the role so challenging. Think about it—leaders need to be bold and cautious, strong and humble, objective and empathetic, tough and compassionate, and we could make the list much longer.

So even though almost everyone would agree that accountability is not only a good thing—but an obvious necessity in most areas of life—it's also seen as difficult and dreaded. Before looking at the many positive benefits of courageous accountability, let's examine this paradox a bit further. I think we can reconcile the underlying psychology and philosophies that bring these strong opposing feelings about this powerful word—accountability.

WHY WE RESIST

Reflect on this wall of impediments to accountability. As you read through the detailed explanation of each one, see if you can identify your weak spots.

Pride

This is the kind of unhealthy pride, also known as "hubris" that allows us to inappropriately elevate ourselves above others. Because of an inflated ego, we may think that we're "special" and the rules don't apply to us. Some people seem to think they're so smart or so powerful that they can make their own rules.

Underneath, there may be some foundation for "specialness" based on knowledge, experience, position, or skill, but what emerges in the person's mind is a false narrative that they are above others and therefore can operate independent of the standards expected of normal people. Of course, accountability would require vulnerability and transparency that in time might reveal one's prideful specialness—exposing weaknesses, mistakes and in some cases, illegal acts. The expression "pride goes before a fall" certainly fits when accountability shows up.

Fear

There are a multitude of doubts and fears that can cause "normal" people to want to avoid accountability. Fear of failure—*I may not be able to come through.* Fear of making a mistake, fear of not measuring up, fear it will be too hard, or too risky. There is also fear of losing control, fear of being exposed as inadequate, or even as a phony. Like the issue of pride, our fears may have some foundations of truth, but generally they are blown out of proportion. So, in effect, we have given in to internal lies.

Fear and pride often lead to a downward spiral. When the stakes are high, people lacking courage and commitment may cut corners or break the rules to look good or protect themselves. Fear of accountability is often a blinding force for those who have knowingly violated policy, ethics, and the law. Then when accountability comes lurking, as with the "original couple"—Adam and Eve—they try to hide, cover up, or blame someone else rather than face the music. Watch any toddler and you will see the predisposition to avoid accountability. It's in our DNA.

Laziness

Most of us would agree that many of the more serious issues (others' issues, of course) are related to pride and fear. But there is a more subtle challenge that is inherent in all of us— we have to overcome our natural tendency toward laziness. Scientists now know it's built into our brains to take the easy way out—at least in the short run. Recent studies show that the brain uses upwards of 25 percent of a person's total energy expended each day. As such, it has a default to choose the easiest way to make decisions, accomplish tasks, and solve problems—it's called habit.[6] Consider how little thought it takes to brush your teeth or tie your shoes.

From the outside what may look like laziness, or taking the easy way out, is really the brain following habitual "cow paths" back to the barn. In a sense, this brain default to conserve energy and follow habits and mindsets can be a beautiful thing, driving us toward efficiency and innovation—think elevators and escalators and so many other improvements over the eons.

However, there is also a downside to habits and mindsets—they can be either good or bad—wisdom is not always included. Thus, a part of our problem is that the wisdom of responsibility usually requires us to forego taking the easy way out, so we must expend extra energy. To be responsible means taking ownership; it often requires going the second mile—and ultimately it always requires us to be accountable.

Lack of Experience, Knowledge, and Planning

Some people just don't know how to step out and follow through and are hesitant to be accountable or hold others accountable. Perhaps they've not seen a good role model for accountability. Or it stems from an underlying fear as mentioned above. If this is problematic for you, this book provides a good solution. We're going to walk you through a proven process.

Busyness

Related to laziness and inertia, busyness usually consumes us when we're not living by priorities. We have busy schedules and it's easy to procrastinate. Remember the *elephant*, the *rider*, and the *path* presented by the Heath brothers in *Switch*. Changing the rider (your logic) and the elephant (your emotions) may be too hard. So why not consider changing your environment to change the path. (Use schedules and similar tools, or ask someone to help you be accountable.)

Negativity

If this is your challenge, you are paying a high cost. Emotions are highly contagious and negative ones zap energy and undermine teamwork. So the question is, "What are you willing to do about it?" Begin by reflecting on your attitude to discern the energy that is driving your negativity. What would it take for you to courageously believe in yourself and others in order to move forward, supporting the principles outlined here? Are you willing to follow a proven process to success? Doing so would almost surely give you more confidence in your role and build the trust of others for you as a leader.

A wise person once said that people will continue to follow their old ways until they decide there's a greater payoff by changing to a different behavior. Certainly there is a lot of truth in that statement. So let's look at the positive reasons to choose accountability as a foundational concept of your life and leadership.

ACCOUNTABILITY BENEFITS EVERYONE

You don't have to be in a POW camp to value accountability. All leadership and followership is grounded in our ability to handle responsibility. Accountability is about following a process to ensure that responsibilities are fulfilled. Mike Myatt, Chairman of N2Growth explains, *"Accountability is the lowest cost, most practical, and most productive form of risk management and quality assurance that can be implemented across an enterprise."*[7]

As a leader or even a person who likes to succeed, consider the following advantages in building a culture of accountability:

Keeps the focus on results

- ▶ Requires leaders to clarify goals and objectives and manage the process to achieve them.
- ▶ Requires leaders to stay connected to resolve issues and obstacles as they arise—rather than as disappointments at the end.
- ▶ Provides the best opportunity for excellence in execution.
- ▶ Minimizes broken promises, surprises, and unmet expectations.
- ▶ Yields better outcomes that positively impact the bottom line.

Prepares people to be responsible and successful

- ▶ Uses collaboration and a supportive mindset to insure success.
- ▶ Clarifies standards of both behavior and performance for building a healthy culture.

▶ Facilitates a sense of ownership and responsibility.

▶ Develops people into better performers and helps them realize their potential.

▶ Raises morale and improves retention.

▶ Improves employee engagement.

▶ Develops the next generation of leaders for succession.

Whether you're leading a fighter squadron in Vietnam or working a job in your chosen industry, courageous accountability makes for winners. Accomplishing goals and developing people means...

A win for the individual

A win for you, the leader

A win for the team

A win for the organization

Done right, accountability is a vital part of the growth process to help the individual perform at a higher level. It also increases the odds that the person will find a line of work where his or her talents and passions are best suited. Just as important, you grow as a leader as you gain experience and confidence in doing your part to support others in being successful. Throughout the process everyone grows as you learn to respectfully and candidly hold people accountable for their performance *and behaviors* in the workplace.

LEADERS OWN IT

> *"Accountability means not just being answerable for what you do yourself, but also owning the whole thing; leaders who are accountable take responsibility for the collective effort."*[8]
>
> **Bob and Lyn Turknett,**
> Leadership Consultants and Co-authors of
> *Decent People Decent Company*

The first principle of leadership is that leaders are responsible for everything that happens in their domain of influence. Leaders can delegate authority and responsibility, but they always retain both. As the leader you always own it—you can't blame others when things don't work out.

I've been saying this to leaders as graciously as possible for many years. Leif Babin, former Navy SEAL and coauthor of the bestselling book *Extreme Ownership*, said it even more directly: *"The recognition that there are no bad teams, only bad leaders, facilitates Extreme Ownership and enables leaders to build high-performance teams that dominate on any battlefield, literal or figurative."*[9]

You may not like that statement, but it's the reality that you may be denying. To test their theory, SEAL training managers Babin and his co-author and partner, Jocko Willink, swapped the leader from the last place team in BUD/S[10] training with the leader of the first place team. In a remarkable and telling turnaround, very shortly the last place team became a winning team, proving the point that leadership always makes a difference. That's your job as a leader—to make a difference and you can't do that without a culture of accountability.

There are several leadership consultants who have written excellent books on the subject of accountability. (See Appendix D.) In preparing to write this book, I've read a number of them. They are all well written and very helpful, and thankfully they approach the subject from a slightly different angle from what we're doing here. But there is a consistent message in these books that is expressed well by the authors of *The Oz Principle*. In their third principle of accountability, listen to what these experts say.

> *"When the people you count on fail to follow through and deliver on expectations, there's only one thing to do—apply the third and final principle, the Accountability Truth. True accountability begins by looking at yourself, by holding yourself accountable. The truth is, when things go wrong, there is usually something wrong with what "I" am doing. When you embrace this principle, you harness future outcomes and strengthen your ability to hold others accountable."[11]*

What we're all saying is that you, the leader, must own this process. You are responsible to lead and manage it to bring about success. Most of the time that's going to work, but when it doesn't—look first at yourself. What could you have done differently? When you have done your part well and it doesn't work out, you'll be ready to bring about a positive—though it may be painful—conclusion.

A POSITIVE MINDSET IS CRUCIAL

Accountability should be positive, not punitive.
Like our POW leaders who showed courage and compassion to forgive and restore the reprobates, healthy leaders and teams have a positive mindset about people. Your goal is to do everything you can to help others succeed in their work and develop their potential. It's about accomplishing the mission, while at the same time building the competence and confidence of others. When you do this, even if it doesn't work out, you're in the best possible position to influence the next steps for the person and the organization.

The underlying principle here is that you must believe in them, and you must communicate that in your words, body language, and actions. Or, there is a good chance they will pick up on your lack of confidence, and underachieve. For those leaders who are naturally skeptical, this is going to require a major shift in your mindset. It will take courage to risk believing in people. They need your courage; it will give them courage and faith in themselves.

The process should be proactive, not postponed.
Procrastination is usually the enemy of good leadership. Procrastination can come from laziness, but more often it comes from fear—fear of personal rejection. Or it can be an issue of perfectionism—fear of getting it wrong. The truth is that most fears are anchored in the lies we believe about ourselves or others.

Good leaders plan ahead and influence outcomes, rather than react and play catchup. By believing in yourself and the process of the Courageous Accountability Model™ you can move forward to achieve the mission and develop your people. As you will see in the next section, the model is simple and visual. And we're going to take you through every step—all the way to "Closeout."

LEADERS GO FIRST

From years of experience, we've seen that the most effective way to get people to develop and grow is for the leader to set the example. When leaders commit to grow, and take people with them, it makes development a team project and everyone is engaged.

When leaders are vulnerable, this authenticity builds trust and camaraderie. With the Millennial generation, this point is especially important; they are attracted to collaborative efforts. As the graph above shows, when the leader is growing and their team is growing with them, organizational performance rises and mission success can dramatically increase.

MISSION PREP

1. You may *think* that accountability is a good thing, but how do you *feel* about it? Consider how your emotions are driving your actions.

2. Would your people say they observe that you are committed to being accountable for your words and deeds and for your leadership of others? Would you be willing to ask them? Would they feel safe in sharing truthfully?

3. Where are you procrastinating in an accountability area right now? What would it take for you to be pro-active and courageously move ahead?

Watch Lee's Coaching Clip on this chapter.
Go to EngageWithHonor.com

FOOT STOMPER

Accountability is crucial to success. It requires leaders to go first, setting the example by their commitment to be responsible and accountable to themselves. Though human nature tends to resist it, accountability has many benefits, improving both individual and organizational performance. Accountability works best in a positive environment that focuses on three areas: (1) accomplishing the mission, (2) believing in and developing people, and (3) following through to ensure that responsibilities and commitments are carried out.

ENDNOTES

1   Bill Wiersma, *The Power of Professionalism*, (Los Altos,Ravel Media, (c) 2010-11 Bill Wiersma), 120.

2   Operation Rolling Thunder was the name for the bombing campaign that we were all part of at the time of our capture.

3   Jane Fonda aided the enemy with her tapes encouraging servicemen to not participate in the war. She should have been held accountable, but in an unpopular war, the government lacked political power or moral courage to make that happen. In spite of her damaging words and actions, POWs regularly denounce the nasty emails that circulate about her ratting on one of us. Those are bogus; the information is false, and we condemn these emails as such.

4   The US policy was always to avoid bombing hospitals, schools, churches, and dikes; we flyers had very strict rules of engagement about this. But the DRV propaganda machine daily claimed that was our main effort. They obviously showed Jane Fonda "exhibits" of such destruction. One of our POWs actually saw the communists blow up the side of a hospital, in order to have evidence to show a visiting "peace group" proof of their claims.

5   Ox, Oso, and Curly soon restored their relationships and we all have remained close friends for a lifetime.

6   Art Markman, "Influence People by Leveraging the Brain's Laziness," *Harvard Business Review*, May 29, 2015, https://hbr.org/2015/05/influence-people-by-leveraging-the-brains-laziness

7   Mike Myatt, 2006, A top leadership coach and bestselling author of *Hacking Leadership* (Wiley) and *Leadership Matters...* (2007), a *Forbes* leadership columnist, is a member of the board of directors at the Gordian Institute, and is the Founder and Chairman at N2Growth. http://www.n2growth.com/mike-myatt-bio/

8   Robert L. Turknett & Carolyn N. Turknett, *Decent People Decent Company*, (Mountain View: Davies-Black, 2005).

9   Leif Babin (Jocko Willink and Leif Babin), *Extreme Ownership: How U.S. Navy SEALS Lead and Win*, St Martin's Press, 2016, 55.

10 BUD/S (Basic Underwater Demolition/SEAL) Training. BUD/S is a 6-month SEAL training course held at the Naval Special Warfare Training Center in Coronado, CA.

11 Roger Conners, Tom Smith, and Craig Hickman, authors of *The Oz Principle*, Article: The Three Principles of Accountability by The Authors on June 7th, 2012, https://www.partnersinleadership.com/insights-publications/the-three-principles-of-accountability/

SECTION TWO:

The Courageous Accountability Model

"Accountability is a key factor in management because it is the corner-stone of empowerment and personal growth. If no one is accountable for a project, no one gets to grow through the experience of it."[1]

~ Laurie Beth Jones

WE'VE CONSIDERED the following fundamental principles: (1) honor, (2) the role of standards like those in the Honor Code, (3) the need to constantly be correcting back on course, (4) the role of accountability and (5) the importance of leaders being responsible and setting the example. With that foundation, let's look at the execution steps of the Courageous Accountability Model—the focus for the rest of this book. The graphic below provides a visual to help you follow the critical steps that will take you through the process.[2]

There are many ways to look at leadership. Our company uses several different leadership models, depending on the focus of the discussion. For the purpose of accountability, we believe the model presented here is simple and logical, and it provides a visual that leaders can follow in day-to-day execution. We'll be unpacking the specifics in the next six chapters. The goal is for you to be able to connect the "how–to" explanations with the visual model. And ultimately, we want you to make a habit of reflecting on where you are in the process and what you need to do next.

Before walking through the model, there are two more important points to remember:

1. Over-communicate the message[3]

Communications are the glue that holds the entire model together. As you can see in the model, communications touch every piece. It's the same in real life. Without good communications, the process falls apart.

2. Think linear—then circular

Models are usually shown as a linear process because there is generally a logical flow for explaining the overall course. But few things in life follow a fixed, predictable process. Reality is usually erratic and unpredictable—with things happening chaotically, which often means we have to circle back to square one before moving ahead.

So even though we will present the Courageous Accountability Model in a linear fashion, you need to remember that in real life it doesn't work that way. Like riding a bike, the way ahead is rarely level. The rider has to shift up and down to accommodate the slopes and maximize forward movement. In the model, you may be in the Collaboration phase and realize that you have to shift back to the Clarify stage—in order to re-explain something you thought was completely understood.

Such is the life of a leader. Think of the model as a general flow, knowing that at times reality is going to be much more three dimensional—and you may have to loop back to another level.

The Core

First, there is the core of the model shown as **Character, Courage,** and **Commitment**. Without these fundamentals, the day-to-day tactics of accountability are hollow and subject to collapse. More than simple words, they are critical strategies for excellence and success in your work.

Next is the consistent layer of **Communications** throughout the entire model. Regardless of where you are in applying the model, clear, consistent communication must be the bond that holds the entire process together.

On the left side of the model are the strategic steps of *Mission* > *Vision* > *Values* > *Strategy* > and *Decisions*. Anyone working in a business or organization should be well acquainted with these terms. More than buzz words used in work vernacular, they are important steps to aligning and unifying a team or organization.

On the right side of the model are the practical steps used every day to achieve healthy accountability. Let's do a quick overview of the four steps.

Clarify

It's about making sure that people understand your expectations. This requires having an alignment in your thinking. Think from the highest perspective down to the intricate details that are important for accomplishing the goal. Then clearly communicate those details.

Connect

In the POW camps, we would risk our lives to connect with other POWs—overcoming every barrier thrown at us by the enemy. Connection was essential, but not just for the purpose of accomplishing the mission of resisting our captors. As human beings we needed connection for our sanity and survival. Everyone needs connection to know they are valued and respected.

Collaborate

This may seem like an unlikely word for the accountability process, but it captures the positive, interactive experience needed for successful execution of good leadership and management. If people are working for me, much of it is a team effort. Even though I will be delegating authority and responsibility to achieve goals, I can never give up my responsibility for the outcomes. An effective leader supports his or her people's efforts and facilitates their growth through collaboration.

Closeout

The entire process is designed to get results, to make good things happen. So there needs to be a conclusion, which is usually associated with achieving a good outcome and meeting a deadline. If you have been appropriately collaborating, you know how things are going, and you have intervened if things were not on track. So if all has gone well the closeout is about celebrating.

On the other hand, if all has not gone well, then it's time for a serious confrontation as to why the expectations were not met.

These four steps *Clarify* > *Connect* > *Collaborate* > and *Closeout* are like the vital organs of the body; they are crucial to effective functioning and healthy execution. Mastering them will be a lifelong process. Expect these four steps to take you out of your comfort zone, but that's usually the place of growth. The rest of the book is designed to show you how to employ these practical steps to courageously lead your people and engage with honor.

ENDNOTES

1   Laurie Beth Jones, *Jesus CEO*, (New York, Hyperion, 1995), 217.

2   You can download a version for use at your desk or wall mounting at www. courageousaccountability.com.

3   See Lee Ellis, *Leading with Honor: Leadership Lessons from the Hanoi Hilton*, Chapter 8, "Over-communicate the Message."

FOUR:

The Core of Leadership:
Character, Courage, Commitment

*"Probably no other character trait was so universally identified by our
Founding Fathers as essential to the long-run success of the American
experiment as selfless public virtue."*[1]

~ VADM James Bond Stockdale, USN

AS A COLLEGE STUDENT in the early 1960s, I learned
to appreciate fiction through the pen of Ian Fleming and the
adventures of his cool-operator spy character, James Bond. I
could never have guessed that within a span of five years, I'd be
living in the protective shadow of a "Bondesque" heroic leader
bearing the same name, almost—it was James Bond Stockdale,
CDR USN.

CDR Stockdale was the senior ranking naval officer in our
prison system, and often he was the senior ranking officer in
the camp. Like the legendary character we know as James Bond,
CDR Jim Stockdale was complex, being unique and extraordinary in his breadth of interests and achievements. Stockdale
was a man of the arts and an athlete. He was a craftsman working as a supersonic jet test pilot, alongside the likes of future
astronaut John Glenn. CDR Stockdale was also an intellectual,

educated at Stanford and grounded in the classics. He was a Stoic who, like many great philosophers of the past, developed a transcendent appreciation of suffering—through personal experience. Most important for our cohort in the prison cells of Hanoi, he was a leader of great character, courage, and commitment. He regularly demonstrated those characteristics at such an extremely high level, they would normally only be imagined in epic fictional heroes.

POW James Bond Stockdale   VADM James Bond Stockdale USN

In the spring and summer of 1967, Stockdale was completing year two of what would eventually be a seven-and-a-half-year tour of duty in a formidable crucible of leadership. He was the SRO in Little Vegas, which comprised the primary cellblocks for American POWs in the Hanoi Hilton. It was in this time period when he issued his famous B-A-C-K US[2] policy to give clarity about some behaviors that were and were not okay. These new guidelines—along with aggressive covert communications—brought a renewed culture of higher morale and increased resistance in the camp.

The V did not know exactly how the resistance was evolving so quickly, but they suspected that Stockdale was likely behind it. They set out on a mission to break all communications and find out Stockdale's "schemes" . . . and then break him. In the summer of 1967 they proceeded to torture men systematically with a viciousness that did, in fact, give them the results they wanted.[3] Stockdale was exposed and made to pay dearly over the next five years for his bold leadership.

Shortly after the purge began, Stockdale was moved to the torture chambers and underwent severe beatings, the torture cuffs, and ultimately the rope torture. As in most cases, they forced him to submit and sign confession statements and tape propaganda messages. In early 1968 he was again tortured day after day to confess his "crimes," to divulge his leadership. Then when he was at his weakest point, they arranged for him to play a role in a propaganda film.

Stockdale recognized what they were up to, and when shaving for the taping he took the razor they gave him and shaved part of his head into a reverse Mohawk—cutting his scalp so that it bled profusely in the process. Not to be denied their actor, the V brought him a hat to wear for the filming. Left alone in the interrogation room, he grabbed the stool and beat his face until it was a bloody pulp, so as to make his appearance unusable. This was the Stockdale way—resist, resist and continue to resist, even when forced to submit. He was always trying to deny the enemy any ability to use him against his country. [4]

Stockdale went through torture periodically for the next three years, during which most of his time was in solitary confinement in the infamous "Alcatraz" prison with CDR Denton and nine other hard-line resisters.[5]

CHARACTER–COURAGE–COMMITMENT

The three foundational attributes in the Courageous Accountability Model shown below are character, courage, and commitment. They form the core for any practical steps to healthy accountability.

As I was outlining this chapter, I also happened to be reading a collection of Stockdale's articles and speeches entitled *Thoughts of a Philosophical Fighter Pilot.*[6] By the time I was halfway through the book, I knew that Stockdale had to be the lead story of this chapter; after all, whose leadership could better represent the core of the Courageous Accountability Model™— Character, Courage, and Commitment. These three concepts are vintage Stockdale; he understood and demonstrated those qualities as well as any person I've ever known or read about.

Stockdale's heroes were the philosophers of the ages, and so he well understood the issue of honor—why it was so important and how it was so connected to these three core concepts. As a thirty-eight-year-old fighter pilot obtaining his advanced degree at Stanford, fate gave him the rare opportunity to be personally tutored in the classics of philosophy by the renowned professor, Phillip H. Rhinelander. As a departing gift, Rhinelander gave Stockdale a copy of the *Enchiridion* by

Epictetus—it became a handbook for the aspiring Stoic.

Five years later when Stockdale parachuted into the hands of the enemy, those two thousand-year-old lessons came to life—inspiring him to choose suffering over self-interests and honor over shame. As a senior POW leader who consistently went first into the crucible to do his duty, he earned the right to speak to these core issues of honor. Reflect on his words of wisdom used here to introduce these three core concepts of the Courageous Accountability Model.

Character

...whenever I've been in trouble spots—in crisis (and I've been in a lot of trouble and in a lot of crises)—the sine qua non of a leader has lain not in his chesslike grasp of issues, and options they portend, not in his style of management, not in his skill of processing information, but in his having the character, the heart, to deal spontaneously, honorably, and candidly, with people, perplexities, and principles.[7]

Most of us recognize that good character is the foundation of leadership because it is fundamental to trust—which is the currency of leadership. The problem comes, however, when we just assume we have good character—as almost everyone does. But good character cannot be assumed. Rather, it must be evidenced through courage and commitment when:

▶ decisions are hard.
▶ vulnerability is required.
▶ reliability is needed.

- execution of responsibility is essential.
- fear of failure creeps in.
- ambiguity and uncertainty develop.
- standing up for what we know is right—even when risks are involved.

These and many more situations are always hard. It is sound character that counsels and guides us as we face the challenges of leadership. Leaders are held to a higher standard and that challenge is compounded because we are dealing with our own self-interests, along with the public good of our people—all the while being imperfect ourselves.

After the war, one of Stockdale's favorite quotes from Solzhenitsyn brings to light the character issues we are addressing here.

> *"Gradually it was disclosed to me that the line separating good and evil passes not between states, nor between classes nor between political parties, but right through every human heart, through all human hearts. And that is why I turn back to the years of imprisonment and say, sometimes to the astonishment of those about me, 'Bless you, prison, for having been in my life.'"* [8]

Stockdale especially related to this attitude, and most of the POWs I know understood that we were stronger, better men for having suffered to do our duty. At the 40th anniversary reunion of our return, several of us were chatting, and we all agreed that we would never have chosen to be POWs, but we would not have it any differently.

The senior POWs were not perfect, but they were authentic. They knew they had to be because they could not hide the fact that they made mistakes, nor the reality that they could be broken. It happened time and again at the hands of the skilled torturers who were employed by our enemy. Our leaders were vulnerable, freely admitting their plight when they could not live up to the full letter of our then understanding of the "big four" of the POW Code of Conduct. No one could do that, yet always—sacrificially—they were doing their best to live and lead in the spirit of the code.[9]

The best leaders are not only strong, but they also are humble. Because of human nature, we are more likely to find these two highly attractive characteristics at odds, rather than coexisting in the same person. It's difficult—almost counterintuitive—for those who want to appear strong to also be humble. But those who possess authentic inner strength are often set free from worrying about themselves, resulting in humility toward others. Remember, people are attracted to strength and even more so when there is humility with strength.

We will never be perfect. But when we are confident in our values and in our authentic selves—and when we lead with humility—our character will grow stronger. I think this is what I was trying to say to my family in the letter I wrote to my parents on March 12, 1973, two days before our release (shown in the Introduction and in Appendix G).

Keep in mind that for some people, it's not during the hard times that they are the most vulnerable. Quite often it is success that lowers our guard. Stockdale liked to quote Francis Bacon who said, *"Adversity doth best induce virtue...while luxury doth best induce vice."*[10]

Since we can't be perfect, we must always be guarding our

character. Like flying formation or navigating, it's all about correcting back before you get too far out of position or drift too far from course. That's where accountability comes along to be our guardian companion.

Our character requires accountability to stay loyal to our values. Usually we are not strong enough to guard our character alone—we need a team around us to support us in the effort. This was essential in the camps. With rare exception, our leaders would reach out to their brain trust before making those tough decisions that involved balancing honor and survival. In retrospect that was probably the mistake that Curly made (in Chapter 3) when he came down too quickly on Ox.

Most authentic leaders recognize the value of accountability to others. In his landmark book, *True North*, Bill George talks about the key role his team of trusted confidants had played in helping him stay on course over a long career.

Peer groups are becoming more and more popular as leaders come to grips with the business risks of being alone, as well as the need for personal accountability. As a technology company owner, Arlen Sorensen was so convicted of this that in 2000 he launched HTG Peer Groups to help fill this role. Here is his take.

> *"Peer groups have a positive impact on their members through an emphasis on open sharing, benchmarking, goal setting, and accountability. HTG is an international community of over 400 experienced IT solution provider CEOs who meet quarterly in small groups to grow their businesses and improve their lives. Over the last four years our member companies have, on average, seen revenues grow 34 percent, employee headcounts grow 39 percent and profitability grow 34 percent. This far outpaces the industry as a whole. The impact of peer groups is multiplied further inside of companies, and outside through the impact on families and communities. Peers matter, and can change not only business, but life!"*[11]

I've had such a group supporting me and cannot imagine walking alone through some of the decisions I've had to make. What about you? Do you have people who can support you and hold you accountable? They can fulfill that role as your guardian companion.

Courage

> *"In Hanoi...One learned that maintenance of moral authority was crucial to minimizing interrogators' gains in the eyeball-to-eyeball, hour-after-hour, one-on-one sessions. You learned that to keep from being had you had to develop a private reservoir of will power, spirit, and moral ascendency from which you secretly drew solace when the going got tough."*[12]

Further clarifying the responsibilities of leadership, Stockdale agreed with Napoleon's belief that in war, the moral is to the physical as three is to one. Stockdale's interpretation reveals the risks in leaders who succumb to fear, saying,

"...failures of management and engineering are tactical shortcomings that can be fixed, but failures of leadership's nerve and character are terminal, catastrophic."[13]

In the POW camps, courage was the currency of leadership. If you didn't have it you could not occupy a seat at the table for very long. Gus Lee, former USMA (West Point) faculty member and leadership author, makes the point this way:

"Courage is the backbone of leadership. It remains the key force and the pivot point around which our other strengths are leveraged, high core values are preserved, and personal and institutional integrity are maintained."[14]

From my experience of working with hundreds of leaders, it is the lack of courage to confront fears that most often undermines leaders. Several years ago we came up with a "courage challenge card"—a business card that serves as a reminder that we must "lean into the pain of our doubts and fears to do what we know is right."[15] We've talked about courage earlier, but you can expect to see it in every chapter ahead, because courage is fundamental to every aspect of leadership—and especially in carrying out the Courageous Accountability Model.

Commitment

> *"The point then is to do nothing shameful, nothing unworthy of yourself. Because if you do, and you are in any way honorable, it will haunt you and corrode your will."*[16]

VADM James Bond Stockdale, USN

This last quote is powerful regarding the role of commitment in leadership. In reflecting back to the previous chapters, we can see how dis-honorable behavior corrodes our will—if it's not quickly corrected. Once we get seriously off course, it's easy to start rationalizing our true commitments.

Think of commitment as keeping your promises and fulfilling your obligations. Commitment is also about loyalty, dedication, faithfulness, and steadfastness. Isn't it exciting to think about working for and with people who exhibit those characteristics? At the same time, when you think about keeping your own commitments, you know it's going to be hard. Don't let fear intimidate you. Remember the example of Stockdale and so many others in the camps; guard your character, be courageous and keep your commitments. Choose honor—choose courageous accountability.

MISSION PREP

1. We've been talking about it for three chapters now. Are you really convinced that guarding your character is going to be a challenge? Are you willing to engage in that battle?

2. Where might your character be most at risk right now? Who on your team is going to support you and hold you accountable?

3. In the past where have you shown courage in the face of fear? What can you learn from that?

4. Are you really committed to your responsibilities and to the people on your team? How do you think others see you in these three core areas of character, courage, and commitment? Would you be willing to ask them to complete a leadership 360 evaluation on you?

Watch Lee's Coaching Clip on this chapter.
Go to EngageWithHonor.com

FOOT STOMPER

Leaders go first and set the example for accountability. This requires a strong core of character, courage, and commitment. Be clear with yourself about your character by establishing your personal nonnegotiables. Then lean into the pain of your doubts and fears to do what you know is right. Don't forget to engage a team of peers to help you in this battle.

ENDNOTES

1   James Bond Stockdale, *Thoughts of a Philosophical Fighter Pilot*. (Stanford, Hoover Institution Press Publication 431, 1995). 74.

2   See more on the BACK US policy at *research.policyarchive.org/11815.pdf*, 19.

3   This was the same purge (Stockdale Purge) that made it so difficult for us to communicate when we arrived in Little Vegas in the fall of 1967. The purge was so effective that we never received any camp policy except for the brief encounter with Risner until the older POWs moved in next door at Son Tay in November 68.

4   This story is drawn from the author's previous book, *Leading with Honor: Leadership Lessons from the Hanoi Hilton*, Chapter 5, "Fight to Win."

5   For more on Stockdale and the men and life at Alcatraz, read *Defiant: The POWs Who Endured Vietnam's Most Infamous Prison, the Women Who Fought for Them, and the One Who Never Returned*, Alvin Townley.

6   James Bond Stockdale, *Thoughts of a Philosophical Fighter Pilot*. (Stanford, Hoover Institution Press Publication 431, 1995).

7   Ibid 31-32.

8   http://www.goodreads.com/author/quotes/10420.Aleksandr_Solzhenitsyn

9   After the war, we learned that the original writers never intended that we resist answering any question other than the big four of name, rank, service number, and date of birth. It was meant that we were required by international law to give that rather than we were allowed to give only that. Beyond that we were to do the best we could to resist the enemy.

10 Op. Cit., Stockdale 6.

11 Interview with Arlen Sorensen, March 2016. For more see http://www.htgpeergroups.com/

12 Op. Cit., Stockdale 38-39.

13 Op. Cit., Stockdale 203-204.

14 Gus Lee with Diane Elliott-Lee, *Courage: The Backbone of Leadership*. (San Francisco, Jossey-Bass, 2006), 159.

15 For more on the Courage Challenge Cards see www.leadingwithhonor.com/ Download or purchase copies of the Courage Challenge Card at LeadingWithHonor.com.

16 Op. Cit., Stockdale 51.

FIVE:

Clarity Begins with the Leader

"Provide clear expectations when you make an assignment to team members. You can't hold people accountable after the fact; you have to lay the groundwork from the beginning."

~ Stuart R. Levine[1]

CLARITY IS ESSENTIAL, BUT NEVER EASY

In ancient times military leaders feared that someone would sound an "uncertain trumpet" and the soldiers would not know whether they were to attack or retreat. In an effort to minimize ambiguities in his communications to his generals, Napoleon required that his orders be read to a private or corporal, believing if they could understand him, then his staff would surely get the message.

In the early 1800's one of Napoleon's enemies, Prussian military strategist Carl von Clausewitz,[2] also saw the problems of getting clarity in communication. In his classic book *On War*, he coined the phrase of "the fog and friction of war"—referring to the difficulty in clarifying the ambiguities of battle.

In my recent book, *Leading with Honor*, I dedicated an entire chapter to "over-communicating the message" to emphasize the extra efforts required to gain the clarity necessary for developing a cohesive team. Here we take up the subject in even more depth, in order to emphasize the importance of clarity when building a culture of accountability.

In the POW camps, where leaders were usually isolated and communications were covert and primitive at best, getting clarity on what was happening and how we should respond was often a full-time job. The punishment for getting caught communicating was fierce, yet we took the risks. Without those messages, we would not have had clarity about strategy, expectations, outcomes, and the day-to-day encouragement and support for each other and our leaders. But even when the message came through, a lack of clarity could cause serious problems.

In the fall of 1968 and the winter and spring of 1969, a small group was working on an escape plan at the "Annex," an outbuilding cellblock at the camp called The Zoo. (You have to love the dark humor of the camp names—Hanoi Hilton, Zoo, Briarpatch, Dogpatch, Skidrow, and Dirty Bird, to name a few.) There had been several escape attempts in previous years, but none was ever successful—our teammates had been recaptured within 48 hours. Still, the SRO had agreed to go forward with a plan—given certain criteria that had to be met to afford a reasonable chance for success. Execution of the plan required permission of the SRO; he would make the "go—no go" decision.

After several months the instigator of the plan became impatient. One night when some, but not all of the criteria were met, he decided it was time to go. He was beyond athletic—a gymnast type. So with the help of his cellmates, he climbed into the attic and worked his way overhead—across to the boss's cell—to lobby for the needed permission. It was against his better judgment, but the SRO waffled. He said he "would not give his blessing for the escape," but he did not order him not to go.[3] That was more than enough window for the "escaper" to get what he wanted; his aggressive, dominating personality prevailed. He and his partner headed out that night. Most of the men who knew the situation firsthand believed the instigator's motivation was mainly about ego and glory, with his sincere partner going along to help.

The two were recaptured within a few hours. The instigator survived the beatings and torture, but his partner did not. The feared consequences to others in the camp came quickly. Torture and merciless beatings ensued for days as the enemy tried to extract every detail of the plan—while at the same time beating everyone within the area to terrorize them into submission. The purge spread to the other camps, and within a few days one of my cellmates at Camp Hope (Son Tay) was accused of plotting an escape. He was then tortured and isolated in a small concrete tank for five months.

Of course the decision at the Zoo Annex would have been a tough decision for any leader, but it highlights the need for leaders to have clarity in their own minds and then fearlessly "stick to their guns."

As a leader you must clearly and courageously communicate—especially when people are trying to undermine your best judgment. In the POW camp it was paramount to know how to be clear, when to stomp your foot, and when to say, "Watch my lips!" Getting the attention of the strong-willed personalities could be a life-and-death issue. And if you think about it, the urgency of clear, very direct communication applies in multiple industries—a power plant, a paper mill, or a police force, for example. Regardless of the setting, clarity is crucial and the lack of it can result in severe consequences.

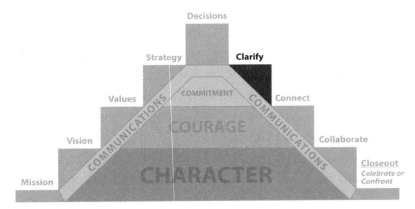

In Air Force professional development courses at Air University, the professors who taught the speaking and writing courses told us to "fight for clarity." Clarifying your message reduces the fog and ambiguity that undermine high performance. Clarity brings understanding, alignment, and positive energy. It opens the door for synergy. Clear communications also help insure: (1) executing consistently with high standards, (2) sustaining your successes, (3) enhancing your credibility, and (4) protecting your brand. But clarity is not easy. There are issues to tackle for both leaders and followers.

CLARITY IS OFTEN DIFFICULT

Leaders must assume that there are "built-in" challenges for followers. Consider the following:

- ▶ Many of us are not good listeners.
- ▶ Some of us don't follow instructions well.
- ▶ It's common to make wrong assumptions about what others mean.

> ► In a progressively "ME"-centered world, many assume the world is the way "I" want it to be.

In any group situation several issues from this list can be at work simultaneously. The reality is that people tend to see and hear from the perspective of their own habits, desires, biases, and mindsets. So if the signals are not clear—and especially when there is a change to an ongoing process—many people interpret subjectively. A good example was a February 2013 revelation from Harvard University, where more than half of the participants in the "Government 1310: 'Introduction to Congress'" class received sanctions for "collaborative" cheating on the final exam. That situation provides a real "Harvard Case Study" on the problems of clarity. It also highlights the attitude of resistance against accountability that seems to be growing in the culture.[4]

When many of the guilty cheaters were kicked out of school for a period of time, there were complaints by some that the instructions weren't clear. They contended that in the past, some of their tests had encouraged collaborative effort. Yet, the instructions for this test were designed to get the students to do independent work/thinking. The instructions clearly stated, "More specifically, students may not discuss the exam with others—this includes resident tutors, writing centers, etc."[5] Still, many students claimed it was unfair treatment, justifying their assumptions because it had been okay to "collaborate" earlier.

Here we see that holding people accountable has become progressively murky, attributable to our self-indulgent culture and the laziness of human nature. This Harvard example highlights the need to intentionally clarify and over-communicate your expectations. Otherwise, some people make their own assumptions and then try to shift the blame to someone else—rather than be accountable and face the consequences.

Situations where team coordination is critical are vulnerable for clarity mistakes. A good example comes from the story of a World War II crew. While taxiing to the runway, the copilot was lamenting his sad situation at home more than he was paying attention to procedures. As they released the brakes and rolled down the runway, the captain looked over at him and said, "Cheer up." What the preoccupied copilot heard was the command, "Gear up."

You can imagine what happened when he quickly executed that command—the landing gear collapsed and the aircraft scrubbed to a halt. Not exactly the outcome the captain had wanted from his consoling remark. Hence, today aircraft have a "squat switch,"—a solenoid in the landing gear struts. It prevents the necessary electrical connections for wheel retraction when weight is still on the wheels.

No doubt each of us has encountered problems with clarity, but we need to be aware of the consequences when clarity is missing. Let's take a look at some of the issues when expectations are not mutually understood.

PROBLEMS WHEN THERE IS A LACK OF CLARITY
- ▶ Desired outcomes/results may not be achieved.
- ▶ Mission and assignment failures or at least less than solid performance
- ▶ Wasted time and energy
  - ● People are doing work that is not necessary to the assignment; time and attention are diverted.
- ▶ Disappointment and frustration
- ▶ People go undeveloped.

- ▶ Trust breaks down.
- ▶ Top performers look for a way out.

TAKE RESPONSIBILITY: AVOID THESE OBSTACLES

Let's face it. Clarity is not easy, and there are many obstacles. The first step is for you, the leader, to get clarity about what you really want to happen. Sometimes this is difficult because you really are not sure yourself. Yet, you can imagine the confusion and wasted effort it can cause when you launch someone on a journey for a destination that is still unknown. So what are some obstacles that inhibit leaders from giving clear direction?

Low Priority

Busyness is one of the greatest challenges that leaders face. How do they do their work and still have time to think—and then lead and manage? Providing clear guidance and expectations must be one of a leader's highest priorities.

Unfocused

Some leaders don't take the time to focus and decide what they want to happen—what success will look like. They might be heard to say, "I don't know what I want, but I'll know it when I see it." That's a cop-out when used as a consistent style of management. If they are not sure of what they want, their expectations will be unclear. Or even worse, they will change their expectations. It's discouraging for their people to constantly be trying to hit a moving target.

Lazy

Sometimes leaders are too lax in their approach, figuring that somehow it will get done. They think that if they give a few instructions they can then withdraw from the process, and one day it will all be completed. This rarely works. It usually takes ongoing dialogue to get the clarity that eventually brings successful outcomes for both results and relationships.

Fear

Some leaders resist clarity because they fear the responsibility of holding others accountable—which, at times, means being firm and risking "negative emotions." When expectations are fuzzy, it's often easier to let others "off the hook." And in doing so, we get "off the hook" of holding them accountable. But with clarity, responsibility grabs us by the collar, demanding that we perform our duty.

Manipulation

This is probably a subset of the fear impediment mentioned above, but here the real motivation is to intentionally avoid being too specific. This allows for wiggle room—perhaps for leaders to change their minds later or to distance themselves from a bad decision in the first place. Clarity requires making a decision and taking risks. That can be tough for all of us. All leaders experience feelings of insecurity at times. This is where courage and commitment enable authentic leaders to lean into the pain of their fears and step forward to meet their responsibilities.

REFLECT AND RESPOND

To be honest, all leaders struggle with clarity—either consciously or unconsciously. I have been guilty of several faults on the list above. So we are not trying to label anyone here. Our goal is to recognize and identify situations where we are not being proactive and intentional about getting clarity. Consider these questions to help you take stock of this crucial component of the Courageous Accountability Model.

1. Where have I not been fully clear with others?
   a. What are the issues keeping me from fighting for clarity every step of the way?
   b. What is the energy and motivation behind my lack of clarity? Consider the list of inhibitors above or maybe you can think of other reasons for not being clear.
2. Right now, who might be struggling to fully understand what my expectations are?
3. Who might be making subjective (personally focused) assumptions about what is expected of them?
4. How motivated am I about having clarity in every direction and with each person?

"One key to a lean and fit company is accountability. In other words, clarity about who is responsible for what. Once you can answer that question, you can eliminate the kind of buck-passing and scapegoating that accompanies bureaucratic irresponsibility"
Howard Putnam,
Former CEO, Southwest Airlines[6]

GETTING CLARITY AT ALL LEVELS

The process of clarity starts at a high level and becomes progressively granular. Since I have an aviation background and most people understand using altitudes to indicate levels of abstractness and detail, we'll do that here. Remember, these levels are completely arbitrary and are solely for the illustration of areas that need clarity. They form a good framework for discussing the significant responsibility of leaders to make sure things are clear.

On the left side of the Courageous Accountability Model, you'll see several overarching, organizational steps that lead to better clarity. They greatly influence the effectiveness of the courageous accountability steps on the right side of the model.

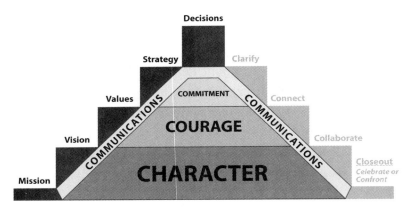

100,000 FEET - MISSION, VISION, AND VALUES
Stephen Covey reminded us of a powerful principle:

 "Begin with the end in mind."

We would do well to follow this maxim at every step of the accountability process. Whether you think of mission, vision, and values as the beginning, the end, or the foundation, these three concepts are a good starting point for all organizations and leaders.

In the POW environment our mission, vision, and values were outlined in the Code of Conduct. They could be summarized in three words: "Return with Honor." With our Code and an occasional line or two of interpretation by senior officers like Risner, Stockdale, Denton, and Guarino, we knew enough to carry out our basic duties and be accountable—even when isolated from the group. The same principle applies in any organization.

Values and Accountability Are Intricately Connected

Most leaders can get their mission and vision defined without too much trouble, but they may fail to clarify the values piece. First of all, it takes time and reflective energy on concepts that can seem "soft" or "fluffy" to results-oriented leaders. I hear things like, "Oh yeah, we all know what our values are," or "Why should we spend time on that? It doesn't make us any money." In Jim Collins' first leadership blockbuster, *Built to Last*, he points out the enduring qualities that come from having a core ideology made up of core values and a sense of purpose—beyond just making money.

Unfortunately, it's also true that some senior leaders resist clarifying values because of a deep fear that if they put it in writing, then they have to live by it—and that may be hard. What if they fail? None of us is perfect and no one wants to look bad and be called out for not living his espoused values. But when you are authentic, you have the courage to walk in transparency and vulnerability—even calling yourself out when you make a misstep. From experience I can say that it's very freeing to accept that you are not perfect and even more so to drop the pose of acting like you are perfect. That vulnerability also builds trust. Think about it—freedom and trust—that's a two-fisted payoff for being authentic.

It's also not unusual to find that what are deemed to be

organizational values are not the leader's deeply held values at all. If they were really solid values in their hearts, they would be passionate enough about them to do their best to live up to them.

Clarifying and systematically living your values requires overcoming ambiguity and taking risks. That's why courage is central to every step of leadership and especially to the accountability process. C.S. Lewis put it very simply:

 "Courage is not simply one of the virtues, but the form of every virtue at the testing point."

Though some values may look and feel soft and others may seem hard to live by, they have the inertia and gravitas of a moving freight train—giving momentum to carry an organization through good times and bad. They provide a good template for self-management at every level, which is one of the keys to developing high performance teams.

Knowing your mission and vision is powerful because they give purpose and focus to your efforts. They bring clarity around which individuals and teams can align and devote their energies toward common outcomes. Moreover, strong core values added to the mix give the effect of glue to further bond individual behaviors to the culture.

Looking back at the Courageous Accountability Model shown earlier in this chapter, you'll see that the entire left side of the model is all about getting Clarity in Mission, Vision, Values, and Strategy in order to make the Decisions that will be executed. Shown below is our alignment model, highlighting how these pieces are brought to play in a team meeting.

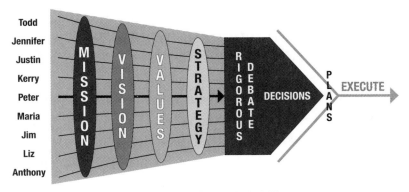

Leadership Alignment Model™

Clarify > Connect > Collaborate

This Clarify and Align graphic illustrates how mission, vision, and values provide parameters within which any issue can be discussed, debated, and decided upon. With clarity about the basic assumptions and ground rules, a team has an aligned frame of reference for debating issues and enabling better decisions with increased buy-in. The end result is a clear understanding of why the decision was made and the message that will be used to communicate the decision. Most importantly, this due diligence process enables the leader to give clarity for execution.

100,000 Foot Mission Prep

1. Do you have clarity on your mission, vision, and values?
2. Do those at the lowest level of your organization have clarity on these areas?
3. Do you use your mission, vision, and values to help your team align for decisions and execution?

50,000 FOOT STANDARDS – INDUSTRY, PROFESSION, AND ORGANIZATION

At this level you will need to be clear about the standards of the industry or profession—as well as how those have been interpreted in the organization. For example, the military has very different standards from Congress, nuclear power is vastly different from the media, and retail would be different from the airlines. Each of these areas has its own culture and expectations of what works well and what does not.

If there is a lack of clarity of expectations around standards and good processes, problems arise. For example, in recent years the NFL has had to deal with serious locker room hazing, child abuse, spouse abuse, and "Deflategate." This series of bad behaviors and ethical issues has sent them scrambling to clarify standards of behavior for players and teams across the league.

Few professions are changing faster than medicine. In the past, physicians were often expected to be treated as gods, never to be questioned or challenged. Now there is a seismic shift happening to move from a physician-centered culture to a patient-centered culture. A new standard of accountability—payments based on outcomes and not just numbers of patients—means that the entire team of caregivers must work together, using evidence-based medicine to provide the best care possible. Moving toward these new standards and a different model is not easy, and old traditions are hard to break. Eventually, however, everyone will benefit from greater professional clarity that aligns the talents of the entire team to serve the patient.

Insuring clarity is an ongoing, never-ending process. New people will always need to be indoctrinated and experienced people will always have to be reminded. As a leader, this is your job.

50,000 Foot Mission Prep

1. Do you have clarity about current industry and professional standards? How well have you clarified them for your team?
2. Have you communicated the standards to the lower levels of the organization? How can you know that they are understood at those levels?

25,000 FOOT OPERATIONS – THE LEADER'S OPERATING PREFERENCES AND PECULIARITIES

I asked one Gen X professional mid-level manager what his first reactions were to the word accountability and his response was, "It's fear." I asked him, "How so?" And he responded, "I'm afraid that my new boss who is located 500 miles away and has little knowledge of the context of my operations is going to come down on me for not meeting some expectation that he's never even mentioned to me. I'm a professional and have a good track record, but he does not know me or my territory very well. And furthermore, he may not understand our situation. He may make assumptions that are totally different from mine." Can you see how clarity would align these two and calm fears?

No two leaders are alike; we have different personalities and different experiences that drive our perspectives. Regardless of what your peculiarities are, it's very important to be clear about them to your team. I have a standard list of eight items that I've used for years to brief people on my specific quirks as a leader. For example, *No "yes" people. If you think I'm wrong, you need to disagree with me early and often until you convince me or I say, "I've heard you and I understand your perspective. If it goes bad, it's not your fault."* This makes it clear that I recognize that others often have more knowledge and better ideas than I do, and I invite input.

Because I'm extremely logic-based, you have to be willing to engage with me to show me a better logic and a clearer picture. But it's also clear that I'm going to own my decision and be accountable for it. Some of the other items include: *I tend to be candid, so don't take my "off the cuff" comments personally. If I'm unhappy with your performance, I'll tell you directly. No gossip. Protect confidentiality. Keep me informed.* My list comes directly from experience. Having your own list and sharing it regularly will significantly increase clarity and collaboration with your people.

At this level there are many other areas of organizational and team policy that need to be clarified. For example, most organizations have a policy of "No marketing or formal written materials go public without a content review and then a final copy edit by someone other than the author." Other areas include internal controls for money-handling, personal internet usage at work, and office space decorations, or perhaps a "no popcorn" microwave rule. At one of my units, we had a procedure for locking combination safes and doors called "Shake, Rattle, and Roll." It was very intuitive, and easy to remember, and virtually guaranteed security when someone was in a hurry to close up shop and go home.

25,000 Foot Mission Prep

1. Have you clarified all your standard operating policies?
2. Are they in writing so people can read them periodically?
3. Do you mention/reinforce them regularly and explain why they are important?

15, 10, AND 5,000 FOOT CONDITIONS – CLARITY ON WHO, WHAT, WHEN AND UNDER WHAT CONDITIONS

"Unless you can point your finger at the man who is responsible when something goes wrong, then you have never had anyone really responsible."
Admiral Hyman G. Rickover,
USN, and Father of the US Nuclear
Submarine Fleet

Everything up to this point has been more static and strategic. Now we are down in the weeds where things are dynamic and tactical, yet we still need both high clarity—who, what, where, and when and as specific as needed to get the job done—and latitude for the "how" part of the task.

GOAL: To Encourage Initiative and Acceptance of Responsibility

Initially, you must identify: (1) what needs to be accomplished, (2) under what conditions, (3) who is responsible for making it happen and (4) what are the potential consequences if it does not happen. This is where forethought by you, the leader, is essential for gaining clarity for yourself and ultimately for launching others into the project. Keep in mind the old saying, "Well begun is half done." Getting clarity about your expectations up front is crucial—and don't forget to ask and answer questions to insure that your people understand.

Be sure to include the purpose of the task or project. The military now uses a concept that applies well here; it's called the Commander's Intent. It's critical that people understand what the boss wants—the desired outcome—and why it needs to be done. How does this fit into our overall mission, vision, values?

Here is where you use your communication skills (and whatever is needed) to paint a picture of your desired outcomes. This is the time to consider not only the objectives, but also natural talents (strengths and struggles)—yours and those of the individuals to whom you are delegating authority and responsibility.

This brings up the issue of delegating authority. If you assign someone a responsibility, you must give them the authority to act to fulfill the assignment. Fearful leaders often miss this point, and then they wonder why people don't show initiative to get things done. You must delegate the authority needed to accomplish the task/mission . . . and that means you have to take a risk.

MISSION PREP

1. Who is going to be assigned a specific responsibility?
2. How good of a match is this assignment going to be for this person or group? (More on this in Chapter 6.)
3. How much experience do they have in this particular skill and the broader related arena?
4. How much interaction—teaching, coaching, monitoring, inspecting, providing feedback—will it take on your part to insure success for this person or group?

This gives you a broad perspective of the levels and types of clarity you need in order to assign responsibilities and authority. Clarity at these levels is so integral to accountability that we'll delve more into these areas in later chapters, where we discuss the details of Connect and Collaborate for successful courageous accountability.

SUMMARY

As you can see, clarity requires a lot of work. Realistically, leaders must go the extra mile to clarify expectations. Whether you are a CEO, a new supervisor, or a parent, it takes energy, focus, thought, planning, and ownership. With clarity you have a sound foundation for decisions, commitments, and responsibility that will ultimately bring accountability to yourself and others. Providing good leadership is always a challenge and bringing clarity to goals and expectations is one of your greatest challenges. Fight for clarity.

Watch Lee's Coaching Clip on this chapter.
Go to EngageWithHonor.com

FOOT STOMPER

Leaders clarify at every level from broad guidance to the specifics needed to do the work. Clarity ensures direction and standards. It shows the way and sets the boundaries and guardrails. Go the extra mile to make sure you and others have clarity at every level.

ENDNOTES

1 Stuart R. Levine, *The Six Fundamentals of Success*. (Currency/Doubleday/Random House, 2004), 108.

2 Carl von Clausewitz, *On War*.

3 Stuart I. Rochester and Frederick Kiley, *Honor Bound: American Prisoners of War in Southeast Asia 1961-1973*, Office of Secretary of Defense 1998, Naval Institute Press 1999, 483.

4 http://leonleeellis.wordpress.com/2013/03/05/on-leaders-and-accountability-part-3-shocking-cheating-scandal-at-harvard-and-clarifying-expectations/

5 http://www.thecrimson.com/article/2012/8/30/academic-dishonesty-ad-board/?page=single#

6 Howard Putnam with Gene Busnar, *The Winds of Turbulence*, (© Howard Putnam, 1991), 69.

7 *War As I Knew It* (1947).

SIX:

Connect: Know Yourself– Know Your People

"As a manager your job is not to teach people talent. Your job is to help them earn the accolade 'talented' by matching their talent to the role."

~ Buckingham and Coffman[1]

THE POWS HELD IN NORTH VIETNAM were very similar in many ways. Some would say we were all indoctrinated into a "military mindset" and to some degree (in a very good way) that's true. Moreover, almost all were aircrew: aviator/pilots, weapons system operators (WSOs), navigators, bombardiers, and electronic warfare officers (EWOs), with a few helicopter crewmen. Having completed this highly specialized operational training meant that we had passed through a number of filters including: academic testing, aviation knowledge and training courses, and proficiency evaluations to insure standardization and quality.

On the surface one could assume that we were peas from the same pod. Yet, the range of diversity was quite broad. Some smoked and some didn't. Some had been heavy drinkers and some were teetotalers. Some were extroverts and some were introverts. Many grew up on farms, but some were from the city.

Those differences could be expected, but there was one that might surprise you. You would think that since all of us were trained military warriors, we would have similar levels of courage and toughness. But in that crucible, facing the enemy all alone, it became clear that was not the case. No doubt, this sample was skewed toward the courage side of the continuum, but there were still differences. The old adage, *"It's not the dog that's in the fight, but the fight that's in the dog"* was clearly evident. Even among these combat veterans some people were just mentally tougher than others. Over time, this was accepted as we saw some men whose ability to take torture far exceeded others.

Major Larry Guarino, POW for more than seven years and commander of the Zoo camp during some of the most horrific years, spoke to our differences in his memoirs saying, *"There are wide differences in people. A very few men, like [Major] Jim Kasler, have the stamina and courage to stick to a hard line during severe punishment and continue to hold out. Most men, although they want to do a good job, will gamely resist the cruelties, but not for very long."*[2] Guarino's comments underscore a key leadership insight that there is a wide range of capacity in people, even among those who have had the same training and experience.

Leaders are usually selected not just for their potential to influence, but to a large degree for their competence in doing the basics of their profession. This means that leaders are often the top performers in their field. As a leadership coach, one of the biggest mistakes I see is that too often leaders assume that others can do what they can do. You don't want to make that mistake. The truth is—you are likely to be much more capable than others in many areas. And if you are smart, you'll realize that in some areas you are less capable than some of your people. The next crucial step in the Courageous Leadership Model is to Connect. In this chapter, we're talking about connecting with an awareness of individual differences.

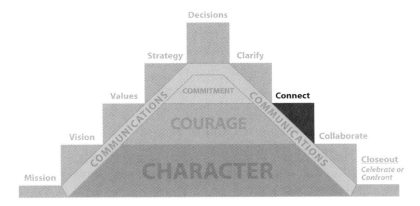

THE ART OF LEADERSHIP

As we move through the model, in the most elemental sense, you could say that following such a process is like science or engineering. But it is also significant that the spectrum of leadership is heavily influenced with many nuances of human behavior. Yes, a logical, step-by-step approach is helpful for understanding the "how" of accountability, but you'll have to engage in the "art" of leadership as well. Why? Because humans are not machines.

Humans have moods, emotions, and spirits that must be lifted. We are each unique and to some degree unpredictable. This "art" aspect can be maddening for some, but to those who really want to excel as leaders, it's the price of admission. It's also one of the challenges that generates such an exciting and rewarding responsibility for leaders.

Many of these human variables are situational and have

to be dealt with in the moment. A detailed analysis of most of these is beyond the scope of this book. But we do want to lay a foundation on the area of differences that is the most predictable—and that area is natural talents. The concept of relating and managing people differently is intuitive for a few people, but for most of us it takes some training and insight, as well as courage and conviction. And as in so many areas in life, experience is often the best teacher.

Early on in my career I picked the wrong person for a job that really required talents for promoting and persuading. Assuming that any conscientious person could handle this short assignment, I picked a highly skilled officer who was naturally humble and averse to promotion and sales. He was a fine officer, but his success in this particular venture was disappointing. In reflection, it was clear that I had not even considered the talents that were needed to successfully complete the assignment. Clearly, I was responsible for a disappointing outcome. I was held accountable. I recovered, but I never forgot that lesson.

> *Expecting someone to be able to do any assignment (or anything that you can do) just because they are diligent and skilled in their primary job is a terrible assumption that will bring disappointment for you and others.*

Later in my career I was in a discussion with a peer about his struggles with one of his people—she just couldn't keep up with her job and frequently called in sick. He was about to let her go. I knew this person and thought she had potential; it was just a misfit. They wanted her to do something that required considerable multi-tasking which was nerve-racking for her. I believed that her poor attendance at work was connected to job stress. As a last resort I offered to try her in my department in a different role. Sure enough, she blossomed and became a very productive worker, filling a niche that no one else on the team could. It was all about finding a job that was the right fit for her.

The moral to these stories is that you must consider the unique talents of your people when you assign work. Otherwise, you may be setting them up for failure. And when they fail, you fail too.

Bottom line—smart leaders learn to identify talents and differences and then lead/manage—and *connect with—people accordingly.*

TALENTS – A TWO-SIDED COIN

Every person has a unique DNA that guides his or her natural behavioral (personality) strengths and struggles—yes, everyone has both strengths and struggles. This knowledge is grounded in science (i.e., it's measureable and predictable, not just "touchy feely"), but the application requires awareness and flexibility to adjust your leadership and management to fit the talents and experience of the individual

In our *Leadership Behavior DNA Assessment* we share both sides of the coin for every individual. Strengths are talents that come easily; we do them by default, almost like breathing. For example, some people are highly organized and naturally talented for the specific details of a project, while others are naturally spontaneous generalists with a wide network of contacts—natural talents for sales and promotions.

On the flip side, struggles come in two shades. First are

the things that don't come naturally. For example, extroverts typically struggle with working alone for extended periods of time. Then there are the struggles associated with overdoing your talents. You may have seen people with talents for organization and accuracy that are rigid, picky, and perfectionistic. Likewise, some people may be very decisive and good at making decisions, but their desire to make every decision can make them controlling and a micromanager—now that's a real bummer for everyone.

We use the noun "struggle" because by struggling with the issue we are able to adequately compensate for (or work around) the weakness—to the extent that others will not view us as having that issue or weakness at all. However, if you don't make the effort to struggle in those areas, they will be weaknesses that will undermine your performance (and leadership).

So, even though this book focuses on general principles and processes of leadership and management, every person is unique, and you can get off track very quickly if you are not considering the real impact of natural behaviors—yours and others. For example, consider how these opposite natural talents will impact you and your people in these areas:

Cooperative and diplomatic ⟷	Decisive and candid
Reflective and focused ⟷	Expressive and adaptable
Fast-paced and challenging ⟷	Patient and harmonious
Spontaneous and general ⟷	Planned and specific
Skeptical and guarded ⟷	Trusting and open-minded
Content and satisfied ⟷	Trailblazing and ambitious
Cautious and safe ⟷	Venturesome and fearless
Practical and orthodox ⟷	Imaginative and original

These are all traits of natural behavior—we are born with them. And though we can learn new behaviors, they rarely are as strong as our natural ones.

If you don't know a lot about your natural behaviors and those of your people, I recommend you complete the Leadership Behavior DNA Assessment.[3] To give you a flavor you might want to begin with the online Leading with Honor Assessment, our free/light report from the full assessment.[4]

With this general overview in mind, let's look more closely at some of the significant areas you need to understand about yourself and those you are working with or managing.

RESULTS-ORIENTED OR RELATIONSHIP-ORIENTED

What is your tilt and what about your people? By our natural design, most of us are inclined to focus on and be more effective at either getting results or building relationships.

About 40 percent are naturally skilled for results (achieving the mission) and 40 percent are naturally skilled for relationships (relating to and developing people). Only 20 percent have significant natural behaviors for both, and when they are under pressure to perform, they lean toward getting results. Think about it.

- ▶ You must get results (accomplish the mission) or you fail.
- ▶ Results get highlighted and rewarded more often than good relationships.
  - ● Senior leaders typically put more emphasis on getting results than taking care of people. Think of the spreadsheets, updates, dashboards, etc. that exist mainly to show progress toward getting results.
- ▶ Considering the points above, it's natural that the higher you go in the organization, the more likely a leader will be results-focused.

The dilemma for all of us is that to succeed over the long haul, leaders have to focus on both sides of the seesaw. That means we have to learn and adapt and apply some skills that are not natural to our DNA. Remember, you are who you are, and you will be the best when you are authentic—you can't reinvent yourself. However, learning to adapt in just a few ways for specific leadership tasks can provide significant leverage for your impact and success.

F-4 Refueling on the Tanker (photo by author)

Think of my F-4 fighter in a refueling operation. At altitude we had to slow down to an uncomfortable level long enough to gas up, but then we went our separate way and back to our normal comfort zone. To adapt like this requires some extra effort and it usually feels unnatural, but it's needed to accomplish the mission. Likewise, learning to adapt to others is essential to managing differences for accountability. But whether we are in the sky, in the office, or at home with family, it takes extra effort and courage to adapt.

Now let's look more specifically at how our ability to understand and manage ourselves and others has a major impact on our ability to achieve courageous accountability.

Results-Oriented Strengths (Mission and Tasks)

As mentioned earlier, 40 percent of the population have a natural drive to get results—these people just want to get things done. Here are some of their strengths:

▶ Big picture, visionary, strategic
▶ Straight forward, give clear expectations
▶ Strong work ethic, good problem-solvers
▶ Decisive, give direction, firm
▶ High standards/goals for self and others
▶ Hold people accountable

So when it comes to accountability, these people would seem to have an edge. They are outcome-focused and they are looking for something to happen, usually sooner than later. They see what needs to be done and don't mind giving direction. Some steps of accountability will be easier for this group than for those who are more relationship-oriented. If you are results-oriented, you may think you have it made, but take a look at the other side of the talents coin. Here are your typical struggles.

▶ Opinionated, not a good listener, discount input from others
▶ May be controlling and not know it
▶ Underestimate work needed to achieve goals
▶ May overcommit what others can do
▶ Sometimes too impatient
▶ May appear coldhearted

Even a novice can see that these attributes are not inspiring, and they can cause a huge energy drain on others. So unless you are aware of how these struggles impact your leadership, you can easily undermine your relationships and your influence over others—totally missing the opportunity you might have to guide them to success. As we'll discuss more in the chapters ahead, part of your role as a leader is to ensure the success of your people. As Ken Blanchard and Marc Muchnick so cleverly related in their neat little fable book, *The Leadership Pill*, making people take more "results" pills is only good for a short-term project or crisis.

Relationship-Oriented Strengths (People and Connections)

This 40 percent of the population naturally notice and respond to people, and they usually enjoy seeing them develop. Many in this group are naturally kind and sensitive. They have radar for others' feelings. Some in this group may be curious about people and mainly interested in just getting to know a new person at a shallow level—sufficiently to get noticed and gain approval. But whether it's one or both of these attractions, these people's strengths are more focused on the people side of the equation. Here are some of the most powerful strengths of relationship-oriented leaders as reported by hundreds of managers we have surveyed.

- ▶ Listen to others' ideas
- ▶ Care for and are concerned about others
- ▶ Encouraging, give positive feedback
- ▶ Trust others to do the job
- ▶ Supportive, lend a helping hand
- ▶ Respect others

But these "people" leaders have their downside as well, and sometimes it's easier to recognize differences by viewing struggles rather than strengths. Here are some of the typical struggles of those whose natural leadership skills are relationship-oriented:

- ► Can be overly optimistic
- ► May lack focus and follow-through
- ► High need to be accepted
- ► May compromise too much
- ► May be slow to confront
- ► Can be naïve and too trusting

These folks may be popular and likeable, but obviously they often have issues in setting standards and holding people accountable. This can undermine their leadership, and high achievers will lose respect for them if underperformers are not addressed. Moreover, everyone wants to be a winner and experience the victories that come from a high performing, functional team. To be successful, relationship-oriented leaders will have to courageously adapt their behaviors to employ some of the skills from the list of "results strengths" presented earlier.

WHICH TILT IS BEST?

Don't go down the false trail that one is better than the other. *You are the best you can ever be when you are your natural self. Accept that both results and relationship-oriented behaviors are essential to good leadership, and then learn to adapt a few new skills to gain a better balance.* With that mindset, you can make the most of your natural self, and then learn to adapt in your weaker area by courageously becoming situationally proficient in some of the strengths from your non-natural list.

Also, keep in mind that the question "Which style is best?" is a tricky question. As I've just said, both leadership styles are essential, but in our consulting and training workshops, we ask people to identify the characteristics of their best leader ever. Typically the higher you go in the organization, the more likely the leaders will be results-oriented. Yet typically, 70 percent of leaders surveyed will respond with a "relationship" attribute like those strengths listed above for that category. How fascinating that results-oriented people valued the relationship strengths of their leaders more than they did their results strengths. It seems that it's all in your perspective. Looking down in the organization, we want results. Looking up, we all want to be valued, listened to and supported by our leaders.

As we approach the idea of accountability, don't go down the path of "I've got to crack the whip." That would be a grave mistake. That mentality is definitely out of balance and fails to recognize the human spirit and the art of leadership. The high achievers mentioned above keenly wanted results, yet they consistently identified relationship traits as what made their best leaders special. It was when they were valued that they felt the most empowered to get results.

HOW WE LEAD AND MANAGE

There are a number of other areas that will be helpful to understand about yourself and others as you engage in courageous accountability. Many of these have some correlation with being results-oriented or relationship-oriented, but not always, and therefore are worthy of consideration. Clearly they will impact how you lead and manage and how others will respond. Consider the following different styles for yourself and then the combinations that you could have with your people.

TASKS VERSUS PEOPLE

You work best alone.

If the individual is like you, then both of you will want to get clarity and then just go get it done. But if the other person is a relational person, it's almost guaranteed that they will want and need considerable interaction with you (much more than you would need in the same situation) in order to get their work done. How will you handle that? Will you be willing to adapt your loner style and spend more time with them?

You work best with people.

If they are like you, you may waste time in small talk and "having fun." If they are different from you and prefer to work alone, they may get irritated at your chatty approach, and start avoiding you.

The great maestros of music conduct so that the drummer, the violinist, and the trumpeter all contribute their best talents to make the concert a success. Likewise, to be a great leader you must be intentional about managing differences—yours and the unique talents of those around you.

MISSION PREP

At this point, you should be getting the picture that people are different, that most people are tilted either toward results or relationships, and that there are both strengths and struggles, regardless of your bent. Now is a good time to get clarity about yourself, so looking back, which way are you more naturally talented? (For a detailed assessment check out the Leadership Behavior DNA™ at LeadershipBehaviorDNA.com.)

Is it Relationships or Results?

▶ Identify three of your strengths from the list associated with your tilt:

1. _Make Concert a success_
2. _Team player_
3. _follow instructions_

▶ Now identify three of your struggles associated with your tilt and identify a counter behavior that you could adopt in order to gain more balance in your leadership.

1. Struggle _Personal influence_
   - Needed behavior _faith_
2. Struggle _To keep going_
   - Needed behavior _patience_
3. Struggle _Spiritual warfare_
   - Needed behavior _pray and read._

Watch Lee's Coaching Clip on this chapter.
Go to EngageWithHonor.com

FOOT STOMPER

Know yourself and coach yourself to do what you need to do to be a responsible, accountable leader. Remember—matching talents to task is critical to success. People are different and good leaders manage accordingly, recognizing individual talents and inspiring their people to succeed, while stretching them to develop to the next level.

ENDNOTES

1   Marcus Buckingham and Curt Coffman, *First Break All the Rules*. (New York, Simon & Schuster, 1999), 95.

2   Larry Guarino, *A POW's Story: 2801 Days in Hanoi*. (New York, Ballantine Books, 1990), 166.

3   http://www.leadershipfreedom.com/DNA/

4   www.leadingwithhonor.com

SEVEN:

Connect with the Heart

*"The goal of many leaders is to get people to think
more highly of the leader. The goal of a great leader is to help people
to think more highly of themselves."*

~ J. Carla Nortcutt

WHEN I ARRIVED AT the Hanoi Hilton prison, I was put in leg irons and cuffs and shoved into a sitting position on a scum-covered washroom floor. At sundown a turnkey appeared with a prison uniform (black pajamas) and indicated I should strip and wash. During the two weeks of the journey north, the fact that I was grubby had never even entered my mind—it had all been about survival.

The bath was invigorating, but the chill of the late November evening and the cold water made for a quick scrub-down. In the days ahead we would encounter another chill that was more ominous, the chilling effects of a communications purge that had painfully swept through the camps a few months earlier.

It had never been easy to connect in Little Vegas and to make matters worse, our cellblock (Thunderbird) was one of the few that had maximum security cells—not even common walls to the cells next door. Isolation was not a surprise, but what we wouldn't know for another year was that during the previous summer the communists had come down hard, attempting to shut down all communications. It was their response to CDR Stockdale's B-A-C-K US policy, mentioned earlier. Now with the guards constantly on patrol, there were almost no opportunities to communicate. The punishment for being caught was extreme, so most POWs were laying low. We "new guys" were isolated in our tiny 6'x7' cell with no connection with others and no knowledge of what was happening in the camps.

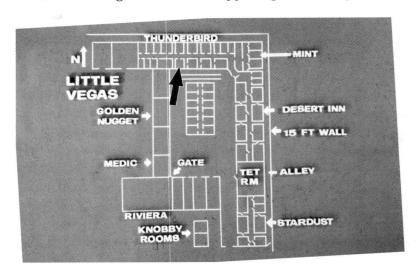

The Little Vegas section of the Hanoi Hilton
The arrow points to my cell in Thunderbird.

One day the men in the cell across the hall diverted the turnkey and his attending guard's attention long enough for their lead risk-taker, Navy Lt. Denver Key, to execute a perfect "message drop"—sliding a note under our door with their four names and shoot-down dates. We were pumped! Finally, we had made contact with other Americans, or more accurately they had contacted us. This icebreaker brought warmth to our spirits that cold first winter. Just to know the names of real people like us, suffering in the same conditions, somehow made life a little more tolerable. That courageous act gave us hope and set an example for us that we could successfully beat the enemy and connect with others.

In that small dungeon, about seven feet above the floor and over my upper bunk (boards fastened to the wall), there was a small window—no glass, only bars—covered with a rattan mat. I began to push the mat away from the wall and eventually bent it back just a few inches, allowing a view around the right-hand edge. I could see a room maybe fifteen yards away that was oriented at 90 degrees to our cellblock. One day I noticed that during the turnkeys' siesta, they had left the shutters open—allowing me to see into this room now being used as a cell. My heart skipped a beat; there stood an older man. He looked haggard and worn. But when I cleared my throat and got his attention, a smile stretched across his face like a sunrise sweeping across the plains of Texas.

Lt. Col. Robinson Risner USAF

Over the next few days I learned that this was Lt. Col. Robinson Risner (USAF), senior ranking POW over all the camps. Risner was legendary as a Korean War hero, ace pilot, and military leader. Now he was the man in charge in the worst hellhole one can imagine. Because of his courageous leadership and resistance, he had been tortured several times and had just come out of 300 days of isolation in a completely dark room.[1] We had heard him screaming out in nightmares, followed shortly thereafter by the yell of guards waking him up and telling him to "Shuddup," "Keep silence."

As we began to communicate—via words slowly spelled out by tracing letters with one finger on an open palm—Risner's countenance lifted; his energy seemed to surge; he was thrilled to have this first new connection after being hidden away for so long. And in a similar way, we were moved to have this first connection with our senior leader, a genuine hero of the highest order. His example and story gave us hope and showed us we could make it as he had—living courageously one day at a time.

There are many good books about the POW experience, and they all have much in common because of the similar experiences we endured. When our stories are compared, the most common threads are about our longing for connections, the risks we took to make them, and the joy we received from human contact.

WHAT DOES CONNECTION LOOK LIKE?

The human spirit is designed to live in community. Being connected is a fundamental need that we all share, but most of us take our connections for granted. Let's look at some of the fundamentals of connection.

A realistic mindset about humanity is essential to being a good leader. Dealing with people and human nature—including their issues—is a key part of what leaders do. However, there are many managers who would love their work if they only had to work with machines and software programs and didn't have to deal with people and "their problems." But, leaders need to lead people and people have deep desires, passions, and long-ings—and especially feelings and emotions, both positive and negative. The obvious point is that when emotions are flowing in a positive direction, there is energy and creativity and pro-ductivity, but when they are negative, it's draining, as though an electro-magnet was sucking the energy out of everyone in range.

At their core, humans are wired for love—to love and be loved. Love is the strongest connection, and for those of you who are feeling this is too "touchy feely," let me challenge you to put your old mindset aside for a bit. Here is the truth. Warriors fight and die in combat mainly for the love of their buddies and their own survival. We've all heard of the "Band of Broth-ers," but unless you have been there, you can't understand this unique bond.[2] Often this military bond is stronger than the family bond.

Much of the problem with love is the word itself—one word that can bring up so many disparate images. We love being at the beach, we love our cars, we love to travel and eat out, we love our friends, we love our families, we love and make love to our spouses. While English uses that one word for a hodgepodge of meanings, the Greek language has four separate words for love. There is:

- ▶ Philos (friendship between equals),
- ▶ Agape (charity, as in God's love for man and man's for God),
- ▶ Storge (love of parents for children), and
- ▶ Eros (sexual passion).[3]

So at this stage of the model, perhaps we need a word other than love to describe our relationship with our teammates. I am advocating here that we use the word "connect." When we say "connect" we are acknowledging that humans seek strong bonds and deep connections. As leaders using this model, we want the Connect step to be connections of the heart—ours to others.

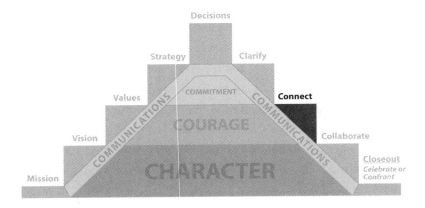

Let's look at some ways that humans desire connection. We want to be:

- Seen and noticed.
- Understood—heard and known.
- Respected and cared about as a person.
- Valued and appreciated.

These are powerful actions that resonate positively in our hearts and stimulate good endorphins in our brains. When we experience these connections we feel energized, inspired, and fully alive. Recall the attributes of great leaders listed in the previous chapter and how often people remembered the relationship attributes of their best leaders over the results attributes. The most frequent response by far was "they listened to me." That one simple act is the most powerful for connection because it speaks volumes about a person's value. Thus, listening is the most appreciated of all "connecting" behaviors. How ironic that it's usually the most difficult skill for leaders and more so as you go higher up in the organization.

Some people naturally resist connection because it feels soft and is tied to emotions. Connecting with a person does in fact touch their emotions—that's the whole point. We are talking about emotional energy. Much of our energy comes from emotions, and the more we can influence those emotions to be positive, the better for performance. Think about what happens when you lift someone's spirit, energize them, and give them a feeling of confidence, importance, value, and purpose. These emotions are touching the deepest human needs. They bring freedom from the doubts and the little lies they believe about themselves. People are inspired to reach beyond themselves.

So if you "feel" uncomfortable with this soft stuff, let me challenge you to reframe this concept and adopt a different mindset. Connection is powerful for energizing people, and as a leader you can capitalize on that fact to improve the performance of others. If you want to get more and better results, learn to connect. If you want to be even more effective, you must learn to connect to the entire scope of emotions—yours and others.

Even though Daniel Goleman and many others have been teaching us about emotional intelligence for nearly twenty years, it's still difficult for some personalities to connect with their own emotions—let alone notice those of others. It isn't that they are bad people; we know from assessing hundreds of thousands of people that it's their DNA. About 20 percent of the population have almost no natural radar for feelings (emotions), and in fact are turned off by this "soft-sounding stuff."

I was called in to coach a CEO who had been in the position for more than a year, and he still had no connection with his executive team. He knew nothing about them and told me that "it was not natural for him; he was just not good at that sort of stuff." I challenged him that good leaders must have relationships, and suggested that he could be much more effective with his people if he connected with them—at least at a minimum level.

Knowing he was very task-oriented, I set up a spreadsheet with the names of his seven reports down the side. Then I negotiated with him to come up with five things he needed to know about them in order to connect and understand them better. We discussed how he might go about this: coffee meetings, lunch, breakfast, stop by their office for a chat, etc. His assignment was to get all the blocks filled in during the next month. The spreadsheet played to his strengths, and he began to engage to fill in the squares. It was primitive, but we moved the needle and he began to connect.

So if your DNA behavior style naturally shies away from making connections, please trust me and read on. I think you will see that connecting is crucial for leaders, and you can improve your effectiveness and that of your people by making some changes. Again, we are not talking about trying to reinvent yourself—you are who you are. But if you are truly committed to living up to your potential as a leader, you will choose to struggle with your nature in key situations and find a way to bring life to others—via connection.

"Dispirited, unmotivated, unappreciated workers cannot compete in a highly competitive world."
Frances Hesselbein,
Hesselbein on Leadership

WHY IS CONNECTION IMPORTANT FOR LEADERSHIP AND ACCOUNTABILITY?

Connection encompasses many of the functions of leadership. Let's look at some of the elements of connection.

Communications—how often have you heard these expressions?

- ▶ We didn't connect.
- ▶ The connection failed.
- ▶ We are not on the same frequency.
- ▶ He does not understand me.
- ▶ She was disconnected from her people.
- ▶ *You just don't communicate.*

You get the point. We all know that connections are critical for communications, which are the vital media for inspiring, clarifying, collaborating, celebrating, and confronting—just to name a few. These actions are essential for leadership and for any relationship, for that matter.

Trust

Trust is the glue for leaders and their teams. Leaders must go first in giving trust. (Since results-oriented leaders are naturally skeptical, this is a big challenge.) The best way to build trust is through understanding, respect, and acceptance (accompanied by your own vulnerability). And there is no way you can get through that progression without connecting.

Feedback

The feedback loop is a special type of communication, and to be effective it requires a good connection. We all want to know how we are doing. And both encouragement (giving an emotional push) and correction (guiding back to course) require feedback.

Employee Engagement

If you are familiar with this buzzword expression, you know that it has legs. There is a large body of research revealing rampant low employee engagement. It highlights the enormous costs in productivity, profitability, performance, and workplace satisfaction. The evidence shows that there are significant economic, physical, and psychosocial benefits of having an engaged workforce.[4]

In its most basic sense, engagement is about leaders being connected to their people. Gallup's data makes the case that emotionally engaged customers bring an increase of 240 percent more to the bottom line. And the way that you get engaged customers is to have emotionally engaged employees.[5]

When people believe in their leaders and feel valued and important, their work has meaning—to the mission and to them personally. That's the essence of connection.

> *"The way your employees feel is the way your customers will feel. And if your employees don't feel valued, neither will your customers."*
> **Sybil F. Stershic,**
> *Taking Care of the People Who Matter Most: A Guide to Employee-Customer Care*

Retention

Connection, feedback, and engagement are the building blocks for retention of high performers because these all communicate valued relationship. In Buckingham and Coffman's classic book, *First Break All the Rules: What the World's Best Managers Do Differently,* they highlighted this point saying,

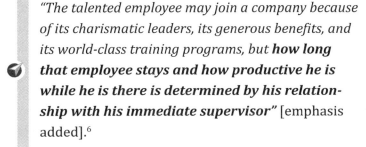

> *"The talented employee may join a company because of its charismatic leaders, its generous benefits, and its world-class training programs, but **how long that employee stays and how productive he is while he is there is determined by his relationship with his immediate supervisor"** [emphasis added].[6]

SENIOR LEADERS NEED TO CONNECT WITH THE ENTIRE ORGANIZATION

Senior leaders typically are not able to connect *personally* with every individual in their organization, but they still need to relate in powerful ways. Recently, I met Maggie DeCan when she spoke to our Atlanta CEO Netweavers group. Her story provided a great example of how this connection can be made.

After working in other industries, Maggie began her career with The HoneyBaked Ham Company in 2002 in HR. In late 2009 she took over as Senior VP of Operations for the Georgia division. With the ongoing fallout from the banking crisis and the ensuing recession, it was a tough time for most companies in her industry. HoneyBaked Ham experienced these economic challenges and had to lay off employees. The company's 2010 Employee Engagement Survey indicated that trust needed to be rebuilt. On the heels of one of the toughest times in its history, Maggie knew that the company and culture needed to change and someone needed to go first—*in situations that require trust, someone must go first.* She knew that it was important to show employees her human side by telling her story and she did just that.

At an employee-wide meeting Maggie shared her story. She explained that even though she had been "successful" at work and had more than 2500 "connections" in her contacts, her career came at the expense of friendships. Moreover, the tough times they were experiencing in the company were not the first she had seen. Her mother committed suicide before she was a year old, and her father died on Christmas Eve when she was just seventeen. There had been challenges and infertility issues in marriage, and she had struggled with lifelong guilt, blaming herself for the loss of her mother. Through it all there had been lapses in her faith.

When Maggie told her story, employees were able to see her heart; they saw her authenticity and humility through her struggles. Telling her story served to elevate trust and followership with employees. Her vulnerability and authenticity were attractive. She could relate to the pain her employees were experiencing with the economy and their insecurity at work.

She connected emotionally, and her story leveled the playing field, drawing them in.

As a result of Maggie's transparency, there was a deeper connection with her team, company results improved, and employee engagement increased. Now under her leadership as President and Chief Operations Officer for the entire company, HoneyBaked Ham has expanded. Maggie said, "The company changed, at least in part, because I changed as a leader."[7]

"Leaders either shed light or cast shadows on everything we do."[8]
Kevin Cashman

RECOGNIZE THE BARRIERS TO CONNECTING

Connecting can be difficult for many, so it's helpful to see some of the potential barriers we face. Truth be told, most of us will have to overcome more than one of these barriers in order to be the leader we want to be—and the leader that others want to follow.

A Transaction Mindset

Recognize that leadership is not just a marketplace exchange— you do your work and I'll make sure you get paid (or promoted). That's certainly an element of life and work, but connection requires more than your head—it requires your heart.

Introversion

Connecting in a meaningful way requires a degree of social energy. Social introverts are de-energized by having to engage with lots of people. Communicating in this way is especially difficult because it is more about the heart than the head. As with the CEO client who used the spreadsheet, many introverts will do well to make connecting a task that is checked off, especially until they form a habit and see the real value that it's bringing to their leadership.

Extroversion

These folks love to connect—at least at a surface level—for fun and attention. But being a giver to the other person and connecting with *their* welfare in mind may be a struggle. Learning how to focus on intentionally investing in others can help extroverts overcome the tendency toward self-focus and ill-timed entertainment.

Highly Results-Focused

Leaders whose DNA behaviors are naturally results-oriented struggle with connection. Some of this is related to introversion mentioned above, but more so, it's their preference for logic and the lack of any "emotional radar" in their natural makeup. Connection feels "touchy feely" and these folks have *strong feelings* about avoiding feelings. This is usually an area of high pay-off for results-oriented leaders. Learning to connect with the hearts of others will bring a significant increase in their leadership influence.

Needy and Insecure

This barrier is about baggage—being a taker and not a giver. We all have some areas of insecurity, but most of us have gained enough healing to become self-aware, learning how to begin to focus on others—and not solely on ourselves. Needy, insecure leaders can suck the life out of the workplace and their behaviors can certainly shortcut opportunities to make meaningful connections with others. Often they are unable to help themselves. They likely will need a strong leader above them to demand more healthy behaviors, which often means referring them to coaching or recommending therapy.

Fear

Fear is the most devastating emotion for leaders. It can either be like dynamite or a termite, but it is usually at the root of most failures that we face or don't face. That's why a central theme of this book is courage. Only when we face our fears and move toward them are we able to fulfill our responsibilities as leaders. By being courageous we can succeed and help others flourish. Don't let fear prevent you from connecting. Move forward and just do it.

Too Busy

Some of you were waiting for this one—thinking this was your "hall pass" for not connecting. Before we approve your "too busy" excuse, please review the first six excuses listed above to make sure the real barrier is not there. If your closest match is "too busy," let me offer one more that I personally experienced.

Ignorance

When I was a flying squadron commander, I was very busy. In addition, I'm sure that several of the barriers above also came into play. But in reflection, I've realized the main reason that I failed to connect with a guy named Alfred was that I was ignorant about this need for connection as a leader—at least in my conscious mind. Let me explain.

Alfred was one of our Captain Instructor pilots whose flight room was on the other side of the building from my office. Alf broke his leg and was put on crutches. I didn't stay on top of the situation and his flight commander was busy as well. Alf's medical condition restricted him from flying. They ran out of meaningful work for him to do on the flight line and instead of keeping him engaged with our team, he gradually stopped coming to work on a regular basis.

A month or so later an older pilot from another squadron came to me and told me that he had been at a party downtown and noticed that some folks were indulging in drugs. He got out quickly, but not before noticing that our sidelined captain was participating in the action. Given that information, I called the OSI (NCIS of the Air Force) and they investigated. Within a few weeks they had evidence that it was not only drug use, but sales. After a court martial we sent the captain to the federal prison at Leavenworth, Kansas.

Looking back I can see that we made a big mistake in not connecting with this young man and making sure he was kept busy within the fold. It's true that he was not my direct report, but he was in my flock, and I take responsibility. As I said earlier, consciously I did not think much about the situation, but there had been a check in my gut. Rather than ask his busy flight commander, "What are we doing with Alf?" I just avoided the situation, hoping it would all work out.

The captain was a bachelor and alone. I did not let him know how important he was to the squadron and to me personally. That was a hard lesson to learn about connecting. I don't want to have to plead ignorance ever again. So let's be alert. Don't allow people to drift; they need to know and *feel* certain that they are not only accountable, but they are cared for.

MISSION PREP

1. Reflect on your best leaders. How did they connect with you? What would you like for them to have done better?

2. Recall an incident when you knew that you should have connected with someone. How would it have changed the outcome had you done so? What kept you from connecting?

3. Are you intentional about connecting with each of the people on your team? How do you know how well you are actually doing this?

4. What barriers do you need to overcome to grow in your ability to effectively connect with others?

5. What is a vulnerable or personal part of your life that you can share to raise the level of authenticity with your team?

***Watch Lee's Coaching Clip on this chapter.
Go to EngageWithHonor.com***

FOOT STOMPER

Effective leaders recognize that their people are human beings with a deep desire to be known, understood, valued, and appreciated. With this mindset, they intentionally connect with them to ensure inclusion, express appreciation, and show each individual his or her importance to the mission.

ENDNOTES

1 Later when I read Risner's book *The Passing of the Night*, I could not comprehend the anxiety and madness he had fought off for some 300 days and nights in the darkness.

2 Because of this bond, one of the biggest issues of war is PTSD. When soldiers come home they can feel guilt and shame that they made it home when others didn't. And it can put them emotionally off balance if they come home before their teammates whom they know are still fighting and losing arms and legs and lives— while they are at home living the good life.

3 https://en.wikipedia.org/wiki/Greek_words_for_love, Note that some sources cite six Greek words for the word love.

4 http://www.kevinkruse.com/employee-engagement-research-master-list-of-29-studies/

5 http://www.gallup.com/services/178028/next-discipline-pdf.aspx

6 Marcus Buckingham and Curt Coffman, *First Break All the Rules*. (New York Simon & Schuster, 1999), 11-12.

7 Adapted from the author notes and with the excellent meeting summary done by Atlanta CEON Executive Director Patricia Hurston.

8 Kevin Cashman, *Leadership From the Inside Out: Becoming a Leader for Life*, (San Francisco, BK Books, 2008), 19.

EIGHT:

Develop a Mindset for Collaboration

"The key to holding others accountable is to be actively engaged with them."[1]

~ Bob and Lyn Turknett,
Turknett Leadership Group

IN THE POW CAMPS where leaders were frequently pulled out, tortured, and then isolated, collaboration was crucial. Though men like Risner, Stockdale, Denton, and Guarino were highly confident, experienced leaders, they were learning the role of POW leadership on the fly. Under the thumb of a cruel enemy, everyone was stripped to his core—leaders could not pretend to know all or be all-powerful—they were regularly crushed right before our eyes.

At the Son Tay camp, Smitty Harris (our Code Bearer) and Fred Flom (a former star collegiate athlete) were in a health crisis. They had lost weight to the point that they looked like survivors from the concentration camps. Through the crack in our door, we watched in anguish as they crossed the prison yard to bathe or empty their buckets. In a period of months their flesh had melted away until we could count their ribs and see their bones sticking out. It was tormenting to see these gallant men suffering. We felt helpless, and unless something changed their trajectory, they were not going to make it. With lives at stake, it was time to take risks.

Using covert communications, our senior ranking officer (SRO), CDR Render Crayton, consulted with his adjoining cells. Then he courageously issued the following order: "Tell every English-speaking Vietnamese you meet that the camp commander must do something for Harris and Flom, or his superiors in Hanoi are going to be very upset with him about what is going to happen in this camp."

Over the next two days those threatening words surprised and shocked our captors at every cell door. Word spread quickly that the plan had been executed. Our feelings were a mixture of pride and fear—proud to be working together to save our friends and fearful of the reprisal that was sure to come. Evidently the gambit was effective; the V responded with medical help—minimum and primitive, but sufficient. Smitty and Fred recovered and are still thriving to this day. That collaborative effort and subsequent victory were highlights of my 1,955 days as a POW and remain a special memory.

That joint action was the first example of an entire camp overtly collaborating to push back on the enemy. However, our SRO Crayton paid the price for his bold leadership. They crammed him into a tiny solitary storage closet where he remained for months—with no windows and almost no air circulation.

Our cell of five guys was the only occupied one with adjoining walls, so it was our responsibility to keep him connected to his flock. As the lead communicator, I sometimes tapped, but more often used a rolled up blanket (like a doughnut) as a muffler to talk through the sixteen-inch walls.

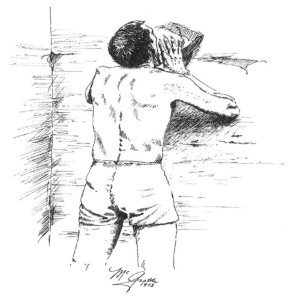

Using a blanket muffler, I could talk through a 16" wall.
Drawing by former POW Mike McGrath[2]

Every day I passed CDR Crayton camp updates and received his policy interpretations. We were his outlet for collaborating with the camp. In the process I learned that this leader—whom I had come to admire greatly—was a GA Tech Yellow Jacket. Being a Georgia Bulldog, it was my first real collaboration with a collegiate arch-enemy—it was my honor to be his neighbor and loyal follower in resisting a *real* enemy.

CDR Crayton, like so many of our leaders, was eager to share his ideas and get input from others before issuing guidance. Though we looked up to them, our leaders' humility leveled the playing field; every person counted; it had to be a team effort. Collaboration with the enemy was anathema, but collaboration among our mates was lifesaving. It was absolutely essential for our mission of Resist, Survive, and Return with Honor.

ENGAGE THE INNER BATTLE TO ENGAGE WITH HONOR

If you feel there are several ongoing themes threaded throughout this book, you are right on—it's been intentional. The goal is to instill in you a mindset that will sustain you in implementing the Courageous Accountability Model. To lead with honor, it's essential that you are sold on the idea that you, the leader, must demonstrate strong character, courage, and commitment.

Moreover, leading with honor and accountability requires a mindset of humility—a willingness to engage in the struggle to balance ego and confidence with concern and caring for others. Like many attributes of leadership, this tension between confidence and humility seems paradoxical and it's rarely easy for anyone. Believe me, as a "take-charge" personality and a former fighter pilot, I experience that tension daily. It is my core values and commitment that propel me to courageously engage in that battle.

Growth is always a struggle because it requires making hard choices to let go of what feels natural, good, and comfortable in order to reach for what we truly want—to live and lead with honor. It's tough because we have to: (1) guard our character, (2) courageously lean into the pain of our doubts and fears, and (3) steadfastly stay committed to our goals and responsibilities. It's a lifelong process and that's why we have to be resilient warriors—engaged in the ever-present struggle between our ego and humility. Growth is not for the faint-hearted.

DEVELOP A COLLABORATIVE MINDSET

As mentioned in previous chapters, having a positive mindset about people is also essential for honorable leadership. Our entire concept of courageous collaboration is anchored in the mindset that people want to succeed; they want to be a part of something larger than themselves; they want to be valued; and they want to count for something. When the leader assumes good will, treats others with dignity and respect, and believes in them, they will be inspired to respond with their best.

We've emphasized the relationship side quite a bit here, but don't get the idea that toughness is not required. Standards are essential to provide the re-enforcing steel needed for any organization that is concerned about accountability. As a sign boldly proclaimed in a corporate headquarters' elevator, "Results count."[3] Isn't that why we count results? And isn't that the reason we need to have a good process for accountability?

*"We found that the most exciting environments, that treat people very well, are also tough as nails. There is no bureaucratic mumbo-jumbo . . . **excellent companies provide two things simultaneously: tough environments and very supportive environments"*** [emphasis added].[4]

Tom Peters,
In Search of Excellence

With this mindset of advancing both a results focus and a concern for people, healthy leaders can engage in a shared process to ensure individual and team success that leads to mission success. Once you have *clarified* and *connected* with people, the meat of day-to-day leadership activity begins in earnest; I'm calling this step in the model *Collaboration*. As we mentioned earlier, the leader must take ownership of this process. Let's look further at the many benefits of collaboration.

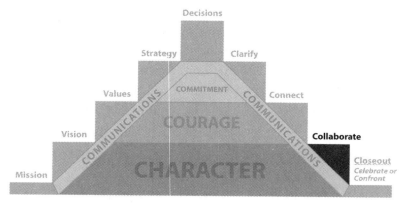

Collaboration Develops People and Gets Results

COLLABORATION FACILITATES ALIGNMENT

From my years as an instructor pilot in the T-38 Talon, I recall the challenge of formation flying as a good example of alignment and collaboration. At 400–500 miles an hour, often only three feet apart, alignment is critical and accountability comes quickly. The leader must take into consideration his (or her) wingmen and collaborate with them so they know what to expect. Sometimes this collaboration is done verbally over the radio, but more often it's done by dipping or rocking a wing, fishtailing the rudder, or using a hand signal. Regardless of the method, the flight lead must let them know what's coming or else there is no way they can stay aligned.

In the same vein, wingmen must work constantly to keep their alignment with the leader. The second you get out of alignment, you are moving away from your leader. And if you do not correct quickly, you no longer will be part of the formation.

Friend and leadership expert Stuart Levine, author of *The Six Fundamentals of Success*, shared in an interview with NBC "Today Show's" Matt Lauer that leaders and followers must work to align their *dashboards*, so they are both looking at the same picture.[5] I love this illustration because it captures three steps of the model: Clarify Connect, and Collaborate—and especially this last one. You really do have to collaborate if you are going to "align your dashboard" with others.

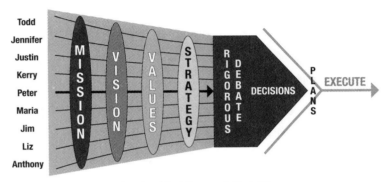

Leadership Alignment Model™
Clarify > Connect > Collaborate

This takes us back to the alignment model and the need for continuing efforts for clarity. Here we see how teams must constantly collaborate, bringing together their various talents and experiences to work through the issues, using rigorous debate to facilitate good decision-making and execution.

"Connect the dots between individual roles and the goals of the organization. When people see that connection, they get a lot of energy out of work. They feel the importance, dignity, and meaning in their job."[6]

Ken Blanchard and Scott Blanchard

IMPROVING TEAMWORK THROUGH COLLABORATION – UP, DOWN, HORIZONTAL

Perhaps your first thought is about collaborating down a level to align with your people. As we've just discussed, leaders and followers must work together to gain similar perspectives on the challenges and solutions for achieving both the mission and the inherent tasks. That is our main focus in this book, and we'll dig into that later in the next chapter. But for overall success, collaboration is needed in every direction.

Leaders must collaborate upward to make sure they are aligned with their manager or board. This could be in strategy, planning, finances, logistics, or even something as technical as cyber security. Reflect on your experiences of both effective and ineffective upward collaboration, and you will immediately notice that without collaboration there will be a noticeable drop in performance. Why? Because negative energy is spent to resolve issues of non-alignment.

The other direction is sideways—in the same plane as your level of responsibility. Without collaboration with your peers, you end up in vertical silos and your success is limited to two directions—up and down. When you collaborate with your peers, you knock down those walls and dialogue flows freely—not only for you, but for those beneath you. When peers collaborate, it frees their people to collaborate and that's powerful for taking an organization to the next level of success.

COLLABORATION GETS RESULTS AND BUILDS TEAMWORK

Almost ten years ago one of my healthcare clients (Northeast Georgia Health System) foresaw a tsunami-like population growth from Atlanta coming toward their coverage area. They knew they had to enlarge their facility and to do that they had to get money. Step one was to get their finances in excellent shape to get the best rates. They decided to cut twenty million dollars from their budget.

Rather than assign a percentage cut to each area, they assigned a task force to each department—made up of people from several departments—to form cross-functional teams to solve the problem. It worked. They made the cuts, got great rates, built the facilities, and never looked back. Today they are the number two rated hospital in the nation.[7]

Strong leadership and great people are obviously driving this success. It's not so obvious from the outside, but if you scratched beneath the surface, I think you would find that the cross-functional collaboration from that budget-cutting exercise played a significant role in launching them on a meteoric trajectory of upward excellence. Collaboration cracked the silos, built trust, and freed managers and employees to work together to succeed at a higher level than they could have dreamed.

COLLABORATION HELPS MINIMIZE RISKS

Most business people know about CRM (Customer Resource Management), but not everyone knows about the other important use of the acronym CRM—Cockpit Resource Management, which started in aviation, and has now been broadened to Crew Resource Management to cover a wide variety of high-risk occupational settings. In the Air Force CRM is a big deal in all multi-crew aircraft because of the need for teamwork and the need to reduce safety risks when there are several "cooks in the kitchen." Unfortunately, some of the overseas airlines were slow to adopt and master a systematic collaborative process in the cockpit.

The accident report from the disappearance over the mid-Atlantic of Air France flight 447 in 2009 highlighted what can happen in the absence of CRM. The mystery surrounding this tragedy was eventually unraveled when the "black box" containing flight data was recovered. It turned out to be a deadly lesson on how a lack of collaboration caused the loss of 228 lives.

The captain had handed over the controls to the second co-pilot and was taking a nap, leaving two co-pilots at the helm. Due to some bad weather, misinterpretations of instruments, and miscommunications in the cockpit, confusion escalated to the point that the co-pilots had no idea what the other was doing with the controls of the aircraft. Unlike almost all dual control aircraft throughout the history of flight, the Airbus 330 controls are not linked, so one pilot cannot feel or see what inputs the other is making—a disastrous example of "dashboards" not being aligned.

They eventually lost control and crashed into the ocean. From his analysis of the accident board report, *Popular*

Mechanics Contributing Editor Jeff Wise concluded: "The men are utterly failing to engage in an important process known as crew resource management, or CRM. They are failing, essentially, to cooperate. It is not clear to either one of them who is responsible for what, and who is doing what."[8]

The idea of CRM has proven to be lifesaving in aviation and is desperately needed in healthcare. In his book *Unaccountable: What Hospitals Won't Tell You and How Transparency Can Revolutionize Healthcare*, Dr. Marin Makary shares insights from a survey he and a group of doctors from Johns Hopkins conducted on teamwork. Describing the results of their anonymous survey of doctors, nurses, technicians and other employees at 60 U.S. hospitals, he says, "We found that at one-third of them [hospitals], most employees believed the teamwork was bad." Those hospitals are probably not where you would want to go, are they?

Other research brings frightening evidence that teamwork and collaboration remains an issue at many hospitals—especially in the operating room where a lack of collaboration can be a life-or-death issue. One study looked at instances in which surgeons operated on the wrong patient, or the wrong part of the body, or left objects inside the patient after surgery. The study found:

 "Compared to other medical errors, the rate of such mistakes in the United States is very low. Still, the study found doctors leave towels, cotton balls, sponges and other surgical equipment inside patients' bodies about 39 times a week, on average. Doctors operate on the wrong body part 20 times a week and the wrong patient, also 20 times a week."[9]

The primary reason for these mistakes is a lack of collaboration—about safety, about processes, and about "evidence-based medicine." It also speaks to the hesitancy of nurses and other operating team members to speak up and confront the surgeons. Collaboration requires a major mindset change for many physicians, but the stakes are high and the evidence is clear—CRM is good for the patients and mitigates risks for doctors and hospitals. Whether it's in aviation, medicine, marketing, or any endeavor, leaders must learn to collaborate. And that includes making it safe for teammates to challenge their leaders and each other when there are problems.

COLLABORATION DEVELOPS YOUR PEOPLE

Good leaders realize they can't do all the work and they must have talented, trained, and motivated people on their team. Moreover, good leaders see the value in developing both the performance and potential of others, and they are intentional and collaborative about that process. They take ownership for the development of others.

As you may have guessed by now, I'm a visual person. Sometimes the only way I can think something through is to picture it in my mind and draw it on a white board. A few years ago, while working on a module of training to help leaders coach their people, we discovered that the word "development" meant different things to different people. To the typical manager, development meant develop for "performance improvement." Of course it does mean that, but in our classes, we were trying to get them to focus on developing the "potential" of their direct reports. To illustrate that concept we came up with the following continuum.

When developing the performance abilities of others, leaders need to use every tool in their kit, to include coaching, collaboration, training, demonstration, and teaching—whatever it takes. But because this development is focused toward results related to the current job, the leader is usually driving the development and thus it can be more instructional in nature.

Development for potential, on the other hand, rests more in the hands of the "coachees," and they need to be more the initiator of development. This type of development relationship is going to be primarily facilitative, but it's still collaborative.

Showing the two on opposite ends of the spectrum is helpful for conceptual discussion. In practice, however, there is a great deal of overlap, and leaders are usually doing some of both. The main point here is that collaboration will be one of the most important tools a leader has to develop others for current performance and for their future potential.

In reading Medal of Honor recipient Staff Sergeant Sal Giunta's autobiography, I was struck by the level of involvement by his leader in providing training and development. The commitment of his Sergeant to make sure that Sal learned how to become a good Team Leader is an example of extreme collaboration that brought extreme success.

> *"Moving to First Squad as Bravo Team leader under Sergeant Gallardo automatically meant that my life was about to become harder . . . He would demonstrate, then ask you to do the same. And then the two of you would work on it together, over and over, until you got it right. He was tireless that way, and utterly unflappable. He was, in short, exactly the kind of leader and mentor I needed: smart, aggressive, demanding."[10]*
>
> **Staff Sergeant Sal Giunta,**
> Medal of Honor Recipient

In a recent article for *HRTech*, my friend Harry Glantz, VP HR for RailWorks, highlighted a way that collaboration can bring together the best contributions of two very different workplace populations. The idea is that intergenerational sharing can be very powerful. Harry put it this way.

> *"The newest technology affords us avenues to share the expertise of the experienced generations with ease by utilizing technology that is so much a part of the DNA of the x's & y's . . . As we manage talent in this manner throughout the organization, employing the best of all generations, we emphasize collaboration and encourage new heights of innovation. We are literally transforming the organization by nurturing and leveraging the best of all segments of our workforce."[11]*

Collaboration can elevate the performance of leaders and followers. Remember, you as the leader should go first. Your example shows the way and sets the standard for team members to do the same.

MISSION PREP

1. Do you have a collaborative worldview? If not, what viewpoints do you need to give up and what new ones do you need to adopt?

2. Looking at the list of how collaboration can help you lead better, choose two areas in which you have the most room to grow.

   ▶ Facilitating alignment

   ▶ Working three dimensionally (360 degrees)

   ▶ Improving results and teamwork

   ▶ Minimizing risks

   ▶ Developing your people

   ▶ Improving employee engagement

3. What can you do to improve your performance in the two areas identified in question 2?

4. Who can be your wingman to support you in this growth effort?

**Watch Lee's Coaching Clip on this chapter.
Go to EngageWithHonor.com**

FOOT STOMPER

 Leading with courageous accountability requires a collaborative mindset toward working with people. Developing your team and guiding them to success is your primary responsibility. The payoff for this hard work is better results, higher morale, better engagement and retention, and next generation leaders who can take your place.

ENDNOTES

1   Robert L. Turknett & Carolyn N. Turknett, *Decent People Decent Company: How to Lead with Character at Work and in Life*, (Mountain View: Davies-Black, 2005), 135.

2   John M. McGrath, *Prisoner of War: Six Years in Hanoi.* (Annapolis, MD: Naval Institute Press, 1975) 37.

3   This was a Fortune 500 company with strong values and a great culture, generous people programs and loyal employees, but they didn't want them to forget that without results, there would be no company and no jobs.

4   Thomas J. Peters and Robert H. Waterman Jr., *In Search of Excellence.* (New York, Harper Collins, 1982).

5   Author Stuart R. Levine discusses his new book *The Six Fundamentals of Success* with NBC News Today Show host Matt Lauer. http://www.stuartlevine.com/our-company/televisionappearances/

6   "Do People Really Know What You Expect from Them?," Fast Company.

7   http://www.nghs.com/northeast-georgia-medical-center-rated-1-in-georgiafor-the-second-year-in-a-row-and-2-in-the-nation

8   http://www.popularmechanics.com/flight/a3115/what-really-happened-aboard-air-france-447-6611877/ by Jeff Wise PM Contributing Editor

9   http://www.livescience.com/25754-surgeons-make-deadly-mistakes.html

10 *Living with Honor: A Memoir of Medal of Honor Recipient Staff Sergeant Salvatore A. Giunta* with Joe Layden.

11 Harry Glantz, "Transforming Human Resources–Brand and Talent Management through Technologies," *HRTech* Oct 2015.

NINE:

Collaborate—Learn to Engage

"Today's 'conceptual age'—when change is happening so quickly and competition is so fierce—requires leaders to be capable of building strong bonds with their teammates."

~ Cory Bouck[1]

AFTER THE SON TAY RAID of November 1970, we moved back to Hỏa Lò (Hanoi Hilton camp). It was the era of the big rooms with more than 300 of us crammed into seven cells of 40-50 men each. For a stretch of eighteen months I was in "Room 3,"—a cell commanded by LCDR Doug Clower.[2] Doug was a distant cousin to Jerry Clower, the famous country comedian of the '70s. They both grew up in rural Mississippi, so they shared some similarities. When you first met Doug, his good sense of humor with his deep southern drawl and clichéd persona could clearly overshadow his brilliance. He was a naval aviator with two master's degrees—Engineering and Meteorology—a whiz at math and physics.

In reflection, I would rate Doug's overall leadership in Room 3 as very effective. Like all leaders, Doug had both strengths and struggles. Some of the more aggressive POWs thought Doug was too compliant with our captors on day-to-day stuff. At the same time he could react quickly to cellmates who challenged him. And like living with many of us with strong personalities, living with him twenty-four hours a day—week after week, month after month—could wear on you.

Nonetheless, during that period of POW history, Doug created a collaborative environment in our cell that made our lives more pleasant and productive. Recognizing there was a lot of talent around him, he divided our group of 53 men into six flights, each with a flight commander. These six leaders became his brain trust. Through collaboration and heated debates (Pat Lencioni's *Creative Conflict*)[3], Doug and his team of leaders consistently hammered out good decisions for charting our way through the minefields of our forced confinement—inside and outside the cell.

Doug's track record of delegating and letting talented people do their thing was brilliant. It was his idea to have an education program to engage our minds and use our time productively. He picked Capt. Tom Storey (USAF) to lead it. Our program was fantastic—probably the best in the camp. In similar fashion, he chose good project leaders and collaborated with them to provide programs for entertainment, spiritual development, choir, physical fitness, escape planning, housekeeping and more. We had a rich life in spite of the very dire circumstances. When we came home, we went our separate ways, but the collaborative spirit that was developed in Room 3 still prevails. We seem to have a better turnout than all the other cells at our NAMPOW reunions, which echoes back to our team's close connection and collaboration.

I'm not sure what Doug's leadership style would have

been outside in "normal life," but the extreme threats and risks in the camps made collaboration an easy choice. It was a choice that enhanced his impact and made our lives better in so many ways. And in the process, the youngest and most junior officer in the room learned a lot. Thank you, Doug, Tom, Smitty, Jay, Gene, Dave, Bruce, Tom, JB, and others whose example of engaging with honor showed me the way. I continue to be inspired by your example.

BE INTENTIONAL – TAKE TIME TO THINK

Skilled leadership requires considerable forethought. You need to be intentional about how you manage yourself and others. In the POW camps time was abundant, and I often noticed the SRO sitting and thinking long and hard, most likely about (1) the enemy threats, (2) the difficulties and dilemmas of resisting and serving honorably, and (3) how he would respond to the daily challenges of being an SRO to a generally stubborn and opinionated group of followers.

In this information age one of the toughest obstacles to being a good leader is busyness. We tend to get so overrun with tasks and information that we don't have much time left to think, to reflect, to evaluate, to plan and then to communicate.

"THINK OR DIE." For nearly half a century those blunt words were the motto for the Air Forces' Squadron Officers School (SOS)—shouting out a warning to the 4,000 captains each year that attended this eight-week course. It was a bold and candid reminder that the leader had better be thinking ahead. The motto has been softened and expanded a bit to fit the culture and now reads:

Think - Communicate - Collaborate

You can see that it still starts with "Think" and how closely the total concept relates to what we are talking about here. Leaders must think, and the higher up you go, the more thinking you need to do—not just about strategy and tactics, but also about the people who are doing the work.

> *"Thinking is the hardest work there is, which is the probable reason why so few engage in it."*
> **Henry Ford**

The questions then come. How will you make time to reflect on how to lead and manage your people? How can you know how well they are doing? Or how well you are doing in leading them? Or how well the mission is progressing? Here are some tips that can help you be more intentional in your engaging.

In my early roles as a leader, being a visual thinker/learner, I used a picture board on my office wall to reflect on each person. Sitting at my desk I regularly stared at each picture, considering where I stood with each direct report and their direct reports. Some days it was just a quick gut-check on how I was feeling about the individual, their productivity, their attitude, energy, and their development.

In another setting I used a notebook with a tab for each person (direct reports or teammates in a cross-functional project). I displayed their job descriptions and a list of the projects, goals and expected outcomes, as well as time frames.

Today there are many more sophisticated ways to track people and their responsibilities. Some people who are more quantitative (objective) might prefer a spreadsheet or dashboard for each person that tracks goal progress and assigns a rating or number to each of these criteria just mentioned. I like having their picture attached to remind me that I'm dealing with people—and not just numbers.

Regardless of your natural style, you need to be proactively and intentionally thinking about your people . . . and that takes time. This needs to be a high priority, however, so find a system that works for you. (See Appendix J for an example.)

Most importantly, trust your gut. Systems and technology tools are a big help, but don't forget to pay attention to your intuition. If you have a feeling that something is not right—pay attention. Don't ignore those feelings. Col. Dick O'Grady, one of my best leaders ever, taught me that in these situations, dig in and either get comfortable that things are okay or take action to get things back on track. This was one of the most important leadership lessons I ever learned.

"When your gut tells you that something is not right, follow your gut feeling; it is right 98 percent of the time!"
Gen. Wilbur L. Creech

LEARN TO ENGAGE

Collaboration requires engagement. Unfortunately, many leaders respond out of unhealthy emotions. Instead of engaging to collaborate, they let negative emotions drive them to either "dominate" or "withdraw"—as presented on the Leadership Engagement Model™ shown below. All of us have made this mistake at home or at work and usually in both arenas. It's the easy way out, but it's not honorable, and it never works in the long run. Look at the emotions associated with the left and right extremes and you'll see why.

Leadership Engagement Model™

WITHDRAW	*ENGAGE*	DOMINATE
• Retreat	• Believe	• Control
• Hide	• Initiate	• Dictate
• Avoid	• Dialogue	• Force
• Quit/Abandon	• Clarify	• Bully
• Go Passive/Aggressive	• Connect	• Manipulate
	• Collaborate	
	• Celebrate	
EMOTIONS:		*EMOTIONS:*
✓ Fear	*EMOTIONS:*	✓ Fear
✓ Anger	✓ *Courage*	✓ Anger
✓ Distrust	✓ *Respect/Love*	✓ Distrust
✓ Pride/Hubris	✓ *Trust*	✓ Pride/Hubris
✓ Pessimism	✓ *Humility*	✓ Pessimism
✓ Shame	✓ *Optimism*	✓ Shame
✓ Guilt	✓ *Self-respect*	✓ Guilt
	✓ *Confidence*	

© 2008-2016 Leadership Freedom LLC

In uncomfortable situations most people have a natural default to either "dominate" or "withdraw," based on their natural DNA. Negative emotions come from the limbic system of the brain and can be quick and strong, making it easy to go to the left or right side responses. Moving to the "engage" column requires a positive mindset and a belief in a good outcome. It requires you to slow down and use the prefrontal cortex of the brain to rationally consider the issues and what is at stake.

Engagement takes a willingness to respect, listen, share logic, discuss mindsets, and stay engaged to work through to a healthy solution. Most of all, engagement requires setting aside or walking through your fears—and that takes a great deal of *courage.* Evidently this is something that didn't happen enough in NASA before the Challenger disaster.

Morton-Thiokol engineers knew that in cold weather there could be failures with the O-Rings on the booster rockets. With unusually cold weather at the Cape, they encouraged a delay in the shuttle launch and warned of problems that might occur. The head safety engineer refused to sign the launch release, fearing O-Ring failure.

Previous delays in the scheduled launch—and knowing President Reagan was going to highlight the shuttle launch the next day in his State of the Union Address—could have given impetus to the ill-advised NASA decision to go. In that situation, it's easy to suspect that pride and fear affected NASA decision-makers. But for whatever reason, rather than engaging and collaborating with the experts, they chose to "dominate." They dictated "press on." And when the launch button was pressed, the consequences of failure began 37 seconds later. The O-Rings broke loose, leading to catastrophic explosions.[4]

Not every wrong choice to "dominate" or "withdraw" has consequences that are so drastic or that come so quickly, but be assured that "dominating" or "withdrawing" will not end well in the long run.

MANAGE YOURSELF AND MANAGE DIFFERENCES

As you prepare to do the Collaborate step on the Courageous Accountability Model, refresh your mind on the players. Consider their talents (strengths, struggles) and communication styles—yours and the other person or people in collaboration with you. A review of the unique personalities (DNA Behaviors) involved will help you prepare. Consider how you will need to manage each person differently, given their unique attributes.

My ability to anticipate how people would respond was greatly enhanced when I began to understand people's natural, hard-wired behaviors and how predictable they really were. People usually default to their "happy place." As Maslow pointed out, we tend to use the tools/behaviors that we know best, ones that have worked for us in the past.

As we discussed in Chapter 6, understanding and using natural behavior enables you to make the *art* of leadership more scientific and logical. Whenever possible, take into account this powerful information to match talents to the task when you make assignments and do your follow-up. With an understanding of talents and individual differences, you will be able to anticipate where people are going to flourish and where they are likely to let you down. We have all had that happen; here's an example.

On a number of occasions, I've had clients express disappointment in one of their direct reports, and they want me to "coach them up" to meet their expectations. A typical example occurred when a hospital CEO wanted one of his senior leaders to change and operate much more aggressively (act more like him). After looking at the individual's Leadership Behavior DNA™ scores and knowing those of the CEO, I showed him their two graphs for comparison. They were more than two standard deviations apart on the key traits needed in the project. I explained that no amount of coaching would enable this person to consistently demonstrate these critical behaviors. I added, "You could do this easily, but the stretch is too far for this person to adapt—especially on a regular basis."

Natural behavior is a key factor in job/performance success, but there are other factors as well. That's why situational awareness (SA as it's now called in the military) is so critical in every phase of leadership. SA requires the leader to stop and think about how best to manage the person. For example, managing an experienced person is very different from managing someone who is a rookie. Here is a short list of SA considerations:

- ▶ Experience, skill, motivation, strengths and struggles
- ▶ Relative information that you may know that the other person does not know
- ▶ Personal situations in life and at home
- ▶ What is your gut telling you?
- ▶ What other sources of feedback do you have to help you weigh the situation accurately?
- ▶ Your relationship with the person

By thinking through these and other situational data points, your logic and intuition will advise you on how best to help this person succeed.

DELEGATE AND GET COMMITMENT

When you assign a task to someone, there is a lot at stake and much of it comes back to clarity. So, fight for clarity and understanding. Be clear about what is expected. It may be a good idea to refresh your thinking from Chapter 5 with emphasis on the 25,000 foot and below levels. Let's highlight just a few of the items that need to be covered when you are making an assignment.

- ► What is the task?
- ► Why are we doing this? What will success look like?
  - ● Provide a concise explanation of the desired end state.
  - ● How do the results relate to the purpose of the organization? (In the military this combination of end state and purpose is called "The Commander's Intent" and it's become a common part of all operational directives.)
- ► What restrictions or Rules of Engagement (ROE) are in play?
- ► What personal biases, politics, or "history" need to be considered?
- ► What are the resources?
- ► When is it due?
  - ● What milestones do we need to reach to know we are on track? Usually it works best to negotiate this out so that everyone feels comfortable.

Ask for questions and promote discussion through this process. And above all, be willing to listen. At the end, you want an agreement—a mutual commitment for the work. To encourage initiative and acceptance of responsibility, be clear that you are delegating responsibility and *authority* to complete the job.

"Effective organizational leaders must delegate authority and support their subordinates' decisions while holding them accountable for their actions."
Army Leadership: Field Manual (FM 6-22)

DIALOGUE – DON'T MICROMANAGE

Having a regular dialogue with your team members can be difficult, but as we have seen already, connection and communication are needed to stay aligned. The diagram shown below represents a mental picture I've used as a tool to help me collaborate.

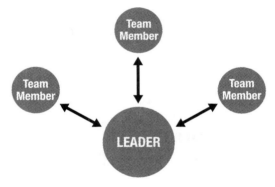

The dialogue process has many uses and varies with each individual and situation. Here are some considerations.

> ► Ask questions. How is it going? What are your concerns about the project? What support do you need? Be their sounding board for a brainstorming session. Pay attention to their responses, tone, and body language. These will tell you how involved they are with the project. Your listening tells them that you are paying attention to their concerns and commitment.

▶ Ask them how they "feel" about the project and their progress. Emotions are critical to energy, and this will tell you a lot about what's going on.

▶ Support as needed. Do they need some coaching or specific training, or perhaps resources or top-cover from you?

▶ Evaluate and encourage. How are they progressing? Are they meeting milestones? If so, give them praise. If not, find out why and ask what it would take for them to get on track.

"Never tell people how to do things. Tell them what to do and they will surprise you with their ingenuity."
General George S. Patton, Jr.[5]

GIVE ONGOING FEEDBACK

Feedback is essential for growth.

If you follow the dialogue model outlined above, you will have regular opportunities to give feedback—not just at performance evaluation time. However, it's so important and so often not done that I want to address the consistent practice of feedback, separately and specifically.

Legendary leadership guru, Ken Blanchard, coined the headline, *"Feedback is the breakfast of champions."* How succinct and true. First of all, affirming feedback provides the energy for growth. An ongoing theme throughout this book is that people have a deep desire to be valued, to know that they count—that they are making a difference. An important part of the leader's role is to connect and help fill that need.

Without ongoing positive affirmation for progress, energy drops. Yet many of us are not very good at this—it's not natural. Rather than go into a lot of "how to" specifics here, I'll just recommend three good sources: *Encouraging the Heart: A Leader's Guide to Rewarding and Recognizing Others* by James Kouzes and Barry Posner, *How Full Is Your Bucket* by Tom Rath and Donald Clifton, and *The Five Languages of Appreciation in the Workplace* by Gary Chapman and Paul White. These books paint a picture of the power of positive reinforcement and offer some good ways to do it.

Feedback needs to be balanced with positive and negative (constructive) insights—both are needed for growth. I heard a nugget on that at a board retreat from my friend Ron Mumme. Ron had been the commander/leader of the Air Force Thunderbirds aerial demonstration team. His dynamic presentation centered around the challenges of being excellent—all the time. He explained how every maneuver they flew in practice and in the shows was graded on a scale of 1-10. To the normal observer they looked to be in perfect formation, but his average score was around a 7. His bottom line was, *"Those who are passionate about performance must be passionate about critique."*

During my flying career we debriefed at the end of every sortie (flight). The good, the bad, and the ugly were laid bare on the table, and there was almost no concern given to rank or position. Flying formation with four high performance jets that are only three or four feet apart can be risky business—accountability comes quickly—excellence requires a constant honing of the skills, and that requires regular feedback. The same principle applies everywhere—those who want to be excellent must learn to welcome feedback and leaders must learn to give it in a constructive way.

Critical feedback always stings.

The one thing that I learned early on is that the slightest negative comment will sting. Even the most confident and successful leaders twinge when they hear they are anything less than perfect.

That's why it's so important that you get your mindset and your emotions in a positive place before engaging to give critical feedback. Formation flying sorties are so interdependent, that they are debriefed with the group, but individual critiques are best done in private—with rare exceptions. Use your relationship capital and your professional credibility as much as possible to assure the person that you are being genuine, and you have their best interest at heart. They need to be confident that you are trying to help them, not cut them down.

So when giving critical feedback, give it some thought and be prepared. These tips will help:

- ▶ Sooner is better than later.
- ▶ Pay attention to:
  - ● timing
  - ● tone
  - ● temperament—yours and theirs
- ▶ Be specific—not general.
- ▶ Be accurate. Get your facts straight.
- ▶ Use objective data where possible.
- ▶ Don't minimize, but don't pile on.
- ▶ Make it developmental—not personal. Your goal is to correct or improve performance or behavior.

There was a great story about feedback in Forbes Online in 2013, giving insight into the leadership of HP CEO Meg

Whitman. To illustrate Meg's character and courage, the article related the situation and impact of her giving feedback to her boss, Tom Tierney, when she had just become a junior partner at Bain Consulting. Tom was a brilliant but domineering leader, yet she went to his office and asked him if she could give him some feedback. He said yes. Forbes tells the story this way.

> *"...Whitman grabbed a felt-tip marker and sketched a giant steamroller on a nearby flip board. "This is you, Tom," she explained. "You're too pushy–you're not letting us build consensus leadership."*[6]

Tierney was stunned. But he eventually absorbed the message and toned down his stridency. All of Bain benefited. "There was a real courage to her," recalls Tierney. "What she told me was a gift. Even though her feedback was negative and unsolicited, it left me liking Meg more."

The story tells a lot about the courage of Meg Whitman and the humility gained by Tom Tierney. She leaned into the pain of her fear to do what she thought was right—even though clearly she was taking a big risk. It also underscores the comment earlier about the need for professional and relational capital when giving feedback—especially up and sideways.

STAY CONNECTED TO YOUR BOSS AND HR

When you see problems that you are not able to solve by coaching, training, or re-direction, you need to do something and not procrastinate. In some situations it may be good to confidentially get a perspective from someone who is not as close to the issue. If your conclusion is that the problem is not likely to abate through normal leader support, then it's time to collaborate with your boss and HR to consider a course of action—a plan designed to get the person back on track.

I've typically found these sources to be especially useful in helping me think things through—to consider what is at stake and what the range of options might be.

If you give it your best shot and it doesn't work, then you will be faced with a real confrontation with a capital C. We'll discuss this more in Chapter 10. Be sure to document the issues and your efforts to help the person solve the problem.

BE COURAGEOUS – IN ALL SITUATIONS

Courage has been a major theme throughout our discussions. It is the backbone that fortifies leaders to: (1) act in the face of fear and adversity, (2) do one's duty, (3) keep your responsibilities, and (4) employ the leadership attributes, skills, tips, and tools we have been discussing. Every person has different fears, but courage is a common element needed by all. Consider this list and identify where you might typically most need courage.

- ► Courage to communicate
- ► Courage to affirm
- ► Courage to support
- ► Courage to confront
- ► Courage to celebrate
- ► Courage to question or challenge
- ► Courage to trust
- ► Courage to let them fail
- ► Courage to patiently coach and teach
- ► Courage to listen
- ► Courage to collaborate and support your people

▶ Courage to adapt and change your mindset when shown a better way
▶ Courage to have fun—without play our hearts shrivel up.

Because courage is so crucial to good leadership (and healthy living for that matter), the wording on the Courage Challenge card mentioned in Chapter 4 has become a mantra for me, "Lean into the pain of your doubts and fears to do what you know is right, even when it doesn't feel natural or safe." (See Appendix H.) I use this often to coach myself toward honorable choices and actions.

MISSION PREP

1. Do you regularly set aside time alone to think about your organization and people?

2. Are you proactively working to keep your team and individuals aligned by pulling issues through the filters of mission, vision, values, and strategy? Are you then engaging in healthy creative conflict discussions?

3. Are you having regular dialogue with your people? Do you know how they are doing? Are they getting support to include regular encouragement and constructive feedback on their progress?

4. Are there areas where you are uncomfortable, resulting in procrastination on decisions or actions? What would it take for you to lean into the pain and courageously engage the issues?

5. Who can be your wingman to support you in this growth effort?

***Watch Lee's Coaching Clip on this chapter.
Go to EngageWithHonor.com***

FOOT STOMPER

Collaboration improves alignment and increases employee engagement. Be intentional and proactive. Take into account each individual's unique style and differences as you engage them with dialogue to support, encourage, evaluate, guide, correct, and give ongoing feedback. It will take courage at almost every step. Be courageous to do your duty, and you will be rewarded with loyal followers and ongoing success.

ENDNOTES

1   Cory Bouck, *The Lens of Leadership.* (New York, Aviva, © Corry Bouck 2013).

2   Fellow POW Doug Clower passed away at age 79, Oct 3, 2010. He was a good friend and a good man. The website below offers a great poem about Doug. http://www.findagrave.com/cgi-bin/fg.cgi?page=gr&GRid=59682968

3   Patrick Lencioni, *The Five Dysfunctions of a Team: A Leadership Fable* (San Francisco: Jossey-Bass, 2002).

4   "Truth Lies and O-Rings," Allan McDonald, and NPR interview with MT Engineer Bob Ebeling http://www.npr.org/sections/thetwo-way/2016/01/28/464744781/30-years-after-disaster-challenger-engineer-still-blames-himself

5   George S. Patton Jr., *War As I Knew It* (Bantam Books, 1947).

6   George Anders, "The Reluctant Savior of Hewlett-Packard," (*Forbes*, June 10, 2013).

TEN:

Closeout: Celebrate (or Confront) and Critique

"Success is nothing more than a few simple disciplines,
practiced every day."[1]

~ Jim Rohn

AS MENTIONED IN CHAPTER 3, the bombing of North Vietnam resumed in the spring of 1972. By October our chief negotiator, Henry Kissinger, thought he had a peace agreement in hand, only to see it fall apart as the communists made a last minute maneuver. Evidently President Nixon understood that power respects power; he gave the okay to "hit 'em hard." The Linebacker II operation was like the earlier one on steroids, raining bombs on North Vietnam's industrial and transportation centers round the clock through much of December 1972.

By the New Year, it seemed their will had been broken. The turnkeys at Dogpatch began telling us that we might go home soon. Our conclusion was similar, but after the many false hopes over the years, we were cautious—"we'll wait and see" was the typical outlook.

On the evening of January 19, 1973 we heard the trucks coming into camp—a lot of trucks—so we knew something was up. The next day we loaded up and headed south; after nine months at the Chinese border mountain camp we were going back to Hanoi. Driving on the roads toward Hanoi in broad open daylight was a sure sign that the bombing had been paused, or more likely stopped. In sharp contrast to the trip up, this time we made reasonable rest stops and were free to walk around. It was a very different feeling from our trip the previous spring. We could almost sense freedom in the air.

A week after we got back to Hanoi we were brought out into the prison yard to hear the news—the war was over and the peace agreement had been signed. The just-signed Paris Peace Agreement required our captors to read aloud in English the protocol for POW release and give each of us a personal copy. The key point was that we would be released in groups over the next sixty days in accordance with the final withdrawal of US troops from Vietnam.[2]

For this momentous occasion, we gathered as a ragtag military formation. When the word that we had waited so long to hear was spoken, not a single person cheered or showed the slightest emotion. There was no celebration—only silence. We turned and headed back to our cells like nothing had happened. That sounds bizarre, so let me explain.

First of all, we were not going to give our enemy a photo op for propaganda. We had experienced too many years of their devious efforts at creating false publicity. The old Hỏa Lò prison museum in Hanoi is now filled with photos of "good food," "good times" and "good treatment"—once a year events that were solely for propaganda. Second, we were still there and having experienced the communists' lying, deception, and lack of honor,[3] we knew the accord could easily fall apart. We were not going to get on an emotional high only to come crashing down in disappointment. No, we would wait and see. In addition, after all those years, we had become emotionally flat, intentionally restricting our feelings to a narrow range—not too high and not too low. Still in enemy hands, for many of us, celebrating with any significant outward expression was beyond the range of our emotional repertoire.

Flying home on the Hanoi Taxi. In this picture, I am in the 5th row, right side.

The celebration did come, when we got airborne in Hanoi, then again when we reached international waters headed outbound, and even more so at the hospital at Clark Air Base in the Philippines.

But the real celebration came a few days later when we were reunited with our families. The joy of being back to family and freedom was deeply meaningful, and hardly a day goes by that I don't celebrate in some small way. Primarily I celebrate by being thankful. I'm filled with gratitude to have survived and now to have such a wonderful life of freedom with my family.

CLOSEOUT – TIME TO CELEBRATE

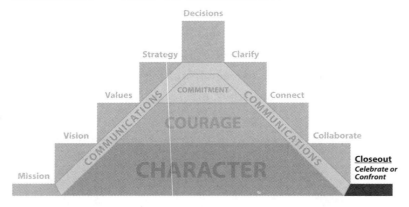

You have followed the Courageous Accountability Model step-by-step and it's worked. Victory has come. It's time to celebrate. Unfortunately, for various reasons, many leaders struggle with celebration.

Barriers to Celebration

► *Baggage from the past.* When we came home from the camps, it was more difficult to celebrate emotionally than I would have expected or wanted. To be honest, I still struggle to celebrate. It's my baggage from the POW experience and part of my ongoing healing process. I've found that I'm not alone. Others struggle with celebration because of pain from a legacy of too much discipline or self-discipline. We must break free from these shackles; else we'll be prisoners of our past. We have to take it head-on and be intentional to work on it.

► *Results-oriented.* In my years of providing leadership development I've seen many people—especially those who are highly "results-oriented"—struggle with celebration. They say, "It's just not my cup of tea." "I don't need it." And to a large degree that's probably true. However, if you are a leader and this is your mindset, please don't let this be an excuse. Reframe your worldview to think about others and what they need, knowing that celebration will in the end bring a better workplace, better teamwork and better results.

► **Fear.** I've had quite a few leaders tell me that they avoid celebration because they *fear* that if they support or promote it, people will let up, performance will go down, and results will falter. Notice the word fear. But aren't leaders paid to take risks and lead others to a higher level—in spite of fear? The antidote is courage. Need I say more?

► **Life struggles.** Someone has said that children celebrate easily, and the older you get the less natural it is. There seems to be some truth in that. Life is serious and it's often a struggle, so it's easy to get more serious as time goes by. The wear and tear of leadership responsibilities can become heavy, but that's a big part of the role of celebrations—to lift our spirits and lighten the load. When we celebrate, it gives us a pause, to make life and work more cyclical.

Have you noticed how nature prefers cycles—think sine curve—and the "ups and downs" of life? Celebration comes as a natural part of the "ups," and without it the highs get lower and the lows get deeper. So let's vow to be more intentional about celebration. Here are some reasons to celebrate and some tips that will help.

Reasons to Celebrate

Regardless of where you are on the celebration continuum, knowing why you are doing it and how it can contribute to your mission is helpful. Celebrating is good because it:

- ▶ provides needed recognition and reinforcement for successful performance.
- ▶ lifts morale and raises energy.
- ▶ reduces stress and lets people relax from the grind.
- ▶ builds esprit de corps, cohesion, and teamwork.

Realistically, there is not much downside to celebrating—especially if it's done wisely. Let's look at how that can be done.

Tips for Celebrating

A momentous payoff has just occurred in your team as you've applied the steps of the Courageous Accountability Model—your team (or perhaps an individual) has successfully accomplished his or her goal(s)! Things have gone well; as their leader, your expectations have been met and possibly exceeded.

So what do you do now? How do you celebrate? How do you affirm success? This is the time for you to come through by being accountable in your role as the "chief celebrator" in the organization. As we've discussed, this may not be part of your natural skills, but you are going to be intentional and succeed in your accountability to follow the model. Here are some tips to help you successfully celebrate.

▶ ***Plan your steps.*** Be clear about what you are celebrating and how you will affirm the achievements. Your goal is to be very specific in your affirmation; before speaking, take time to reflect on what went well and what steps in the process made the work successful. Remember—you want to recognize and "call out" what worked well, reinforcing the mindsets, behaviors, and attributes that you know will yield success again in the future.

▶ ***Be enthusiastic in your demeanor.*** It's been said that communications are 20 percent verbal and 80 percent non-verbal, so your energy, tone, and body language are all going to play a big role in communicating genuine satisfaction. It's true—some people are naturally more expressive than others; so if being low key is part of your personality, then you'll need to stretch your energy and emotions a bit. This may be your courage challenge, but it's one you don't want to fail at. Regardless of where your natural level of enthusiasm falls, you will need to punch it up a notch to show your pleasure at the way things have turned out. A big smile, high fives, and good words of affirmation communicate positive emotions that inspire others with energy for the next challenge.

▶ ***Be fair and consistent.*** We humans have very sensitive egos, and people notice what you are doing for others. They expect you to be at least as excited about their success as that of others. The way to nip office politics in the bud is to take care of the needs of each person individually as you work with them. Almost everyone is searching for validation at a very deep level to confirm that "My work has meaning; I'm making a difference; and I'm valued." Great leaders help people become successful and that means recognizing individual differences and providing affirmation of their unique contribution.

▶ *Consider temperament and natural behavior.* Introverts want to be recognized, but usually in a more private way. Don't make the recognition so public that it's painful. Extroverted, outgoing folks love the limelight—the more public attention, the better. Think this area through and maybe get some counsel. With time and more experience, you will learn what works.

▶ *Consider the next challenge.* Successful people are generally looking for their next challenge, so be ready with a stretch assignment. Always keep in mind that one of your important leadership responsibilities is to develop your people. Be thinking about the next steps in their careers and how you can be preparing them for higher levels of responsibility.

▶ *Celebrate team successes as a team.* The joy of victory lifts spirits and provides a great time to enhance connection and build camaraderie. If organized fun is not your thing—no problem—just delegate it and manage it like any other project. Every team has some people who have a passion and talent for bringing people together to celebrate. You will be amazed at the time and energy they will put into it—and the positive results.

The bottom line is: good leaders know that people love winning. They enjoy the challenge of taking their team over the top, celebrating, and then moving to the next goal and the next victory. Surely we can all take on this challenge. The risks are small and the rewards are high.

MISSION PREP FOR CLOSEOUT: CELEBRATE

1. What about you? Are you reticent to celebrate? If so, which barrier(s) do you need to overcome?
2. Are you providing affirmation and enthusiastic, positive feedback to your folks as they achieve their goals? What could you be doing to better affirm and value your people?
3. Are you willing to ask your folks to give objective feedback on how well you are doing in this area? Ask them, "On a scale of 1-10, how well do you think I'm doing on giving positive feedback and affirming your success?"
4. How about team successes? Ask, "On a scale of 1-10, how are we doing in celebrating as a group?"

CLOSEOUT – TIME TO CONFRONT

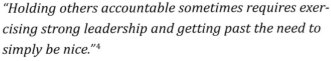

> *"Holding others accountable sometimes requires exercising strong leadership and getting past the need to simply be nice."*[4]
>
> **Bob and Lyn Turknett,**
> Leadership Consultants, authors of *Decent People, Decent Company*

Confrontation can be difficult for everyone—even those who are "tough" often procrastinate dealing with accountability failures. It's generally not in human nature to move toward being uncomfortable, and for most people confrontation is uncomfortable. From experience, I believe that you have to have a mindset that recognizes confrontation as being both the right thing and the kind thing to do—for either unacceptable performance or undesirable behavior. That's why following the Courageous Accountability Model is so important. If you have done that, you have done your part to help the person succeed as a leader. Looking at it through these lenses, you can see it is your duty to all parties to deal with these issues in a kind and firm way. There must be accountability; else there is no honor, and no opportunity for the individual to grow in either performance or potential.

Viewing confrontation from the mission and team perspective, General Colin Powell explained it this way.

> *"Good leadership involves responsibility to the welfare of the group, which means that some people will get angry at your actions and decisions. It's inevitable, if you're honorable. Trying to get everyone to like you is*

> *a sign of mediocrity: you'll avoid the tough decisions, you'll avoid confronting the people who need to be confronted, and you'll avoid offering differential rewards based on differential performance because some people might get upset. Ironically, by procrastinating on the difficult choices, by trying not to get anyone mad, and by treating everyone equally 'nicely' regardless of their contributions, you'll simply ensure that the only people you'll wind up angering are the most creative and productive people in the organization."*[5]

Mission and team come first, but healthy accountability often benefits the individual most. If you think about it, it seems almost cruel to let someone perform in an unsatisfactory manner without confronting them with consequences. Recall that back in Chapter 1 we talked about human nature needing both a carrot and a stick. Negative consequences are the pain that we bring on ourselves when we fail to keep our commitments and meet promised expectations. Leaders must be willing to play their role in that sometimes painful process. This is how we learn; it's how we grow. As Stockdale and Solzhenitsyn counseled (and most of us who are healthy have learned), it is from suffering that we learn the most effectively. One of my Marine POW mates put it this way: *"Pain purifies."*

I still vividly recall a "consequential" event early in my Air Force career. I was a 22-year-old 2nd Lt. going through F-4C Phantom combat training and enjoying it immensely—you might say, "a hotshot in the making." That is, until my commander called me into his office for a serious confrontation. He had been informed that I had bounced a check at the officers' club at another base. I stood at attention while he chewed me out for bringing dishonor on the corps. I knew the rules (this was a real "no-no"), but had been negligent in keeping up with my account balance. The boss made it clear that I was on the watch list and any further instances would bring swift punishment that would impact my performance report and my career. It was painful, but I got the message and it's lasted a lifetime.

"Without consequences, there is no accountability."[6]
Stuart R. Levine,
The Six Fundamentals of Success

As a leader, I learned to accept the responsibility to confront and came to see it as the right thing for everyone. If I had done my due diligence, there was no other healthy, honorable option. My greatest mistakes were the times when I delayed and did not confront and follow through with consequences as appropriate—those were the times I was too fearful, too nice or too lazy, meaning I lacked courage or diligence—or both. From those experiences, I continue to learn and make course corrections to follow the Courageous Accountability Model and engage with honor.

Confront with Confidence and Humility

Once it's clear that confrontation is needed, plan your steps and prepare yourself. You have done it right up to this point, but don't let up now. You need to "Closeout" like a pro. That means taking time to think through the issues logically and emotionally. Logically, you get your facts in order so you can speak objectively about expectations not being met. Emotionally, get yourself in a good place—how would you like to be treated in this situation if you were the other person? Then think through what the reactions might be from the person you are confronting. This should not change the facts, but it may help you know how to present the facts.

Look back in Chapter 9 for tips on giving feedback—specifically the *Giving Ongoing Feedback* Section. They will guide you in your planning for your confrontations. Keep in mind that having a positive presence and a strong and caring presentation is critical to creating a safe environment. First, share the logical facts that lead to the conclusion that expectations/promises have not been met. Then ask a simple and respectful question like, "Help me understand what happened here," or "What do you think happened?"

From here, how you proceed depends on many variables. I've found the book *Crucial Confrontations*[7] to be a big help, and I recommend you check it out. This is an important place in time for you and the other person, and you want to respond like a professional.

If you have determined that consequences are appropriate, don't back off. Decide, make your plan of action, and move forward to do the hard thing, knowing that you are being accountable to fulfill your responsibilities as a leader. Remember that your loyalty is first to the organization, the mission, and the team. You are taking appropriate action to protect others and yourself. That's got to be your focus, regardless of the painful impact on the problematic person.

Confront with a Positive Mindset

Above all, keep in mind that you can't go wrong when you operate with a clear plan and a positive mindset of strength and caring. I can say with all honesty that when Alf (of Chapter 8) was sentenced to federal prison, I cared greatly for him. He was guilty and bore the consequences, and I have no problem with that. But I do wonder what would have happened if we had engaged him more personally and also had been more courageous and diligent in holding him accountable.

MISSION PREP FOR CLOSEOUT: CONFRONT

1. Have you accepted your responsibility to hold others accountable by confronting them when necessary?
2. Is there a situation in which you are procrastinating in holding someone accountable? What will it take for you to move forward with a crucial confrontation?
3. What can you do to prepare yourself for the next confrontation about behavior or performance?
4. Who can provide wise counsel to help you confront in the most effective manner?

CLOSEOUT – TIME TO CRITIQUE THE PROCESS

Regardless of whether you call this "a critique," "a debrief," or "an after-action review," the idea is to set aside a time to discuss the process followed (the Courageous Accountability Model) and the lessons learned for the next cycle. Identify what went well and soak on that a bit. Then look for areas that could be improved on the next time.

Avoid making this a blame game or a time for excuses. As in other situations, this is a time for the leader to go first in owning areas of improvement. This frees others up to "own" their mistakes and to identify opportunities for improvement the next time.

This is also a good time for you to ask for feedback. How helpful were you? What could you do in the future to better lead and manage your people and processes? Finally, be sure to listen for insights into the challenges your people are facing.

You'll want to reflect on those areas and see if there are organizational barriers or trends that you and your manager need to know about.

MISSION PREP FOR CLOSEOUT: CRITIQUE

1. What made this mission or operation so successful? What worked well?
2. What could we do differently next time to improve the process?
3. What could we add or take away from the Courageous Accountability Model to improve our use of it in the future?

Watch Lee's Coaching Clip on this chapter.
Go to EngageWithHonor.com

FOOT STOMPER

Good leaders courageously celebrate individual and team successes. They recognize that celebrating is essential for good morale and employee engagement. They also courageously confront poor performance and hold themselves and others accountable—with clear consequences for poor performance, failed promises, broken commitments, and inappropriate behaviors. Failure to appropriately confront and hold people accountable is an abdication of responsibility that lowers standards, discourages good performers, and deprives poor performers of the consequences that can help them grow.

ENDNOTES

1   http://www.brainyquote.com/quotes/topics/topic_success.html

2   We came home in groups based on capture date—first in, first out. The first group was handed over to the US at Gia Lam Airport on Feb 12, 1973. Another group was released every two weeks. Three more large groups and one small group of sick and wounded were handed over by March 31. I was in the March 14 release, the third large group.

3   With a clear conscience they told us that "truth is that which most benefits the Party"

4   Robert L. Turknett & Carolyn N. Turknett, *Decent People, Decent Company: How to Lead with Character At Work And In Life*, (Mountain View: Davies-Black, 2005), 135.

5   General Colin Powell, Chairman (Ret) Joint Chiefs of Staff Department of the Army, USA, *A Leadership Primer*, http://www.think-energy.net/Colin-Powell-on-Leadership.pdf

6   Stuart R. Levine, *The Six Fundamentals of Success*. (Currency/Doubleday/Random House, 2004), 109.

7   Kerry Patterson, Joseph Grenny, Ron McMillan, and Al Switzler, *Crucial Confrontations: Tools for Resolving Broken Promises, Violated Expectations, and Bad Behavior*, (McGraw Hill, 2005).

ELEVEN:

Troubleshooting Accountability– Tips and FAQs

Disclaimer: This chapter provides insights, tips, and coaching ideas based on years of experience. However, it is not intended to replace legal or HR counsel. The reader assumes all responsibility for its use.

TIPS FOR LEADERS

1. Understand the battle.

Like life, leadership can be a struggle, but if your deep desire is to live and lead with honor, you will be successful—not perfect, but successful. In the POW camps everyone was broken; no person was tough enough to live up to their own expectations of toughness. The way was too hard and we fell short. But our desire for honor was deep and was supported by character, courage, and commitment so we bounced back—we were resilient. It's the same with life—as a person or as a leader.

Life and leadership are hard because we are human; we get off track. We fall short—always have and always will. The key is to recognize it and correct back quickly by returning to honorable practices, doing what you know is right—your duty, your commitments and promises.

The important thing to remember is that you can't let fear or pride deceive you into taking a dishonorable or cowardly action to cover up your mistakes. As my pastor Andy Stanley pointed out when describing how to get out of a mess, "Every mess is a breakdown of virtue . . . You don't get out of a mess by another violation of virtue."[1] That's why pride and fear are your enemies. Pride and fear will take you into a mess and then tempt you to make more wrong choices to try to get out of the mess. Humility is the antidote to pride and courage overcomes fear. With this dynamic duo—humility and courage—you can correct back to course and engage your domain with honor.

2. Start off friendly but lean toward being tough.

When you take over leadership of a team, organization, or even a classroom, be very clear up front about boundaries and expectations. You can always loosen up, but it's extremely difficult to start loose and then tighten up later on.

3. Hire slowly and fire quickly.

Getting the right people on the team is the most important thing leaders do. A behavior problem, a bad attitude, or non-performer can waste your time and suck the energy out of you and your entire team. So make sure that you do your due diligence before hiring. Then if someone does turn out to be a problem, be proactive to get them back on track. If that does not work, follow a sound process to get them out the door. Work closely with your HR managers or get good counsel to make fair, legal, and wise decisions and then take action.

4. Schedule time to think.

The higher you go up the leadership chain, the more demands there are on your time—yet, the more time you should spend thinking. Remember the SOS motto. THINK – COMMUNICATE

– COLLABORATE. If you don't *schedule* time to think, it won't happen. In your thinking time, reflect on the status of people and projects and the objective data that you have available. Also, take time to "feel." Ask yourself, "What am I feeling?" What is your gut instinct about situations and people? Make notes or a list from your thinking and feeling session so that you can follow up. This is how you stay ahead as a leader. If you are not thinking, probably no one is.

5. Increase your awareness.

Awareness is the foundation for all growth and improvement. Self-awareness is crucial for managing and growing yourself. Others-awareness is also important to know how people are doing in their work and in their person (emotions, heart, morale, etc.). With awareness you can manage yourself, respond appropriately to others, and grow in effectiveness.

6. Understand the leadership tightrope.

Most leaders find it difficult to balance mission (results) and people (relationships). From the top, the pressure is for results. At the same time the people working for you are concerned about their agenda, which is more about them. Are they valued? Are they making a difference? Do they have a future? Will they get promoted? What about a pay raise? Is their work contributing to something bigger than themselves? Both results and relationships are important, and if you are not feeling the tension, you are probably not balanced as a leader—one side of your leadership is not going well. Stay engaged with both and let your character, courage, and commitment and the steps of the Courageous Accountability Model help you walk the tightrope between the two.

7. Stay connected to a team of advisors.

My friend Waldo Waldman, fighter pilot and Hall of Fame speaker, has a neat book entitled *Never Fly Solo*. That's great advice. Warriors never fight alone and likewise we all need people around us who care about us, encourage us, and hold us accountable by asking the tough questions. These should be trusting relationships in which you can be completely vulnerable. Most of these should be the same sex, but we do need trusted teammates from the opposite sex as well. Our opposites often see things we don't.

Leadership guru Bill George makes a strong case for having a support team; he's been engaged with his group for more than thirty years. Additionally, he mentions the value of support teams throughout his landmark book, True North—even devoting an entire chapter to "Building Your Support Team."

FREQUENTLY ASKED QUESTIONS (FAQ)

TEAM ISSUES

Gossip
What should I do if I have a peer that is gossiping or talking negatively about another teammate?

Don't join them—either kindly explain on the spot that it's not appropriate, or excuse yourself and leave the conversation. Then ask to meet with them in private and graciously explain that what they are doing is not kind and makes others feel uncomfortable. Moreover, it undermines team unity. Suggest that if they have a problem with someone they should sit down with them and discuss it. If you are the leader of the team, get your facts and meet with the person and cover these same areas—and be sure to firmly let the person know that gossip is unacceptable.

Not Dependable
My teammate shows up late for meetings or doesn't deliver on promises.

Consider recruiting another teammate to go with you to meet with the person and ask them, "What's up?" Not everyone is at the same level of maturity or professionalism, and sometimes people may be going through a rough time personally. Help them identify the problem and a plan to solve it.

If you are the leader and see this, you can move into it in a similar fashion, keeping in mind that ultimately you have a responsibility to help the individual get better as well as a responsibility to the team to discipline those who are not accountable. This is where you walk the tightrope and where you earn your spurs as a leader. For more on teams holding peers accountable, I recommend *The Advantage* by Patrick Lencioni.

Onboarding
What do you do when you get new people on your team and they don't fit in?

This is a good time to proactively apply the Golden Rule—accept them the way you would want to be accepted—openly and respectfully. Take the initiative to get to know them and help them get to know others on the team. Building understanding is the way to build acceptance and trust, and trust is the glue that binds teams together.

Remember, differences tend to divide, but diversity is essential for healthy teams. Embrace the other person's strengths and talents and tolerate their struggles. Like you, they are not perfect. Welcome them and make it work.

MANAGER/BOSS ISSUES

My boss is hesitant to hold people accountable and we have folks on the team that don't carry their weight. What can I do?

Your manager probably lacks courage to deal with the issues. How can you encourage him or her? By approaching your manager in a respectful way, you may be able to help them see the impact of the problem as well as how to address it. Your manager might be relieved to have someone help him come up with a firm and respectful way to deal with the person.

This situation highlights why relationship capital and professional respect are so important. Looking back I can now see that in the POW camps I had much more influence over my leaders than I ever realized. They listened to my suggestions and often acted on them. That's what we now call "leading up" and it's very important. I unashamedly allow my team to influence me. They often see things I don't and I've learned to listen to them and let them help me lead better.

My boss doesn't support my desire to establish accountability with my team. What do I do?

This situation is somewhat similar to the question above, and like so many manager/employee issues, much hinges on the trust that comes from (1) relationship capital and (2) proven professional competence. If you have those two advantages, you can present your case. You can also make it easier for him or her to support you by sharing some of the benefits to accountability described in Chapter 3.

Also, point out that the accountability we are talking about is very friendly and not punitive. It's really about helping people succeed, and when they don't, helping them understand why. Sometimes it will mean they have to find a different work situation where they can be successful. If someone is not succeeding, why would you not want to help them find a place where they can do well?

I've heard many people say that looking back, getting fired was the best thing that had happened to them. It forced them to find their niche where they could really be successful. This would be a good time to refer to the graphic in Chapter 3 showing that courageous accountability is a four-way winner.

My boss has his own, negative micro-managing version of accountability. How can I change it to a positive one?

Recognize that this style is likely anchored in fear or old habits based on what he learned from his boss in his formative years. As in the previous question, the best way to help your manager is through your relationship capital and your professional performance.

Skeptical leaders are logical, and with a proven track record, you can build trust and increase your leverage. Ask him to take a risk on you by giving you some latitude to operate more freely. Then execute and exceed his expectation. Through solid performance and good communications, it's likely that you can build a trusted relationship that will result in more empowerment, though you may have to ask for it.

We have had an old style "nice" culture for a long time, and as we start implementing accountability for higher standards, folks are balking and doing a lot of whining. How can we handle this?

I've seen this firsthand in several companies so I know what you are talking about. First, you have to almost expect this since no one likes change—and especially when they feel it tightening down on their old ways and habits. It's hard, and some people are just not able to make the change. I believe in giving people choices. If they can perform to reasonable standards and not complain, then they can stay—with the understanding that they will have to adapt to the changes in technology and processes that may come. If they want promotions and incentive pay raises, they must pick up the pace. Realistically, it takes about ten years to completely change the culture in an old line company, especially where they have been a protected monopoly like a utility company.

What is my civic duty regarding accountability with public servants/government?

Get involved; actively communicate with your representatives in government. Let them know what you think. Most importantly, be sure to vote. I'm amazed at the number of people who don't vote—that's not good—elections have consequences for everyone.

FAMILY/HOME ISSUES

How can these principles be adapted for my personal life (family, wife, and children)?

Very much the same as described in the previous chapters and in this one. Human nature is the same. The one thing about home life is that we don't always have the power we think we do, and therefore have to lead more by influence and example. That's a good thing, I think. It's just hard for some people who lead by "command" at work (people jump when they speak) to make the adjustment at home—where things need to be collaborative. Of course the collaborative approach generally works best for developing the next generation, both at home and work.

How can I get my children to be more responsible and accountable?

Give them responsibilities and challenges and allow them the opportunity to succeed or fail. Help them learn resilience by being independent and bouncing back from failures. I don't think you can go wrong by following the Courageous Accountability Model outlined in this book. You may have to scale it down a bit, but the same principles apply.

How can I raise my children to be honorable when the culture seems to be going in the opposite direction?

Walk the talk and share with them how hard it is to be honorable and also share the blessings it brings. Download a copy of the Honor Code shown at Appendix B and discuss each of the seven principles. Explain why they are important and how you personally have struggled with them. Maybe take one week and discuss one per night after dinner.

AT THE END, BUT LOOKING AHEAD

We've come to the end, but we would love for the dialogue to continue. Please join in our social media (see reference in the back of the book). We would like for you to share your thoughts and experiences on these questions and the insights regarding honor in this book.

Our goal is to build a growing community that is committed to courageously engaging with honor, leading with honor and being fully accountable in order to prepare the next generation of leaders. Please join us in this noble cause. *It's one of the best ways you can contribute to the ongoing preservation of our freedom and our way of life.*

ENDNOTES

1   http://northpointonline.tv/messages/address-the-mess/messy-er

Epilogue

ENGAGE WITH HONOR

I hope this book has stirred your interest in the idea of engaging with honor. It won't be easy, but the rewards are great. During my years as a POW, it required sacrifice and suffering to live by our Code of Conduct and to do my duty. I have no regrets. The struggle to keep my commitments and return with honor has brought many blessings.

To live with honor is a choice. We can engage in the battle to be honorable or we can violate our values and commitments and reap the guilt and shame that follow. That's a terrible place to be for many reasons, but the most serious may be that our DNA has a built-in tendency to try to hide our transgression—and that usually brings the baggage of more unhealthy choices and behaviors.

Unfortunately, dishonorable "personalities" sometimes rise to prominence and that further clouds our view of honor. After all, they seem to be getting away with it. In Psalm 73, Asaph describes his struggle with this very issue, so it's always been this way.[1]

Fortunately, most of us have an honor-based conscience that usually guides our behavior. But as we've seen, our human nature is easily tempted to look for the easy way out, to make excuses, and avoid accountability.

The only healthy long-term choice is to enter the struggle—to engage in the battle for our character and honor. You see, it really is about choices. In *Man's Search for Meaning*,[2] famous psychiatrist and holocaust survivor Victor Frankl explained this in a simple and powerful way, saying:

> *"Between stimulus and response, there is a space. In that space is our power to choose our response. In our response lies our growth and our freedom."*[3]

So I'm challenging you to engage with honor by choosing to join in this battle to live and lead honorably, to be accountable by living authentically in vulnerability and transparency. Your example will have a powerful influence on others, helping them choose to do the same.

For sure it is a battle. As you become increasingly aware of who you really are and even more so when you take ownership for your full self, it will feel uncomfortable. Your confidence is built on believing in yourself—a good thing—but as you struggle to be authentic and face your imperfections, how do you deal with that discomfort?

This self-awareness and the related struggle that it can bring make us feel vulnerable and we don't like it. But it is in that space of vulnerability that we have the choice and in that choice lies our freedom—the freedom to be an authentic leader who is willing to grow right in front of others. This takes **faith**—believing that you will be better off by choosing to suffer in the moment. And it also takes **courage**—the willingness to lean into the pain of your doubts, fears, and discomforts to choose what you know is right.

ACCOUNTABILITY

I trust that by now you see accountability as your friend, as the healthy way to go. And as the leader, I hope you understand that you have to go first. It all hinges on you. You are the role model, the living example of what honor and accountability look like. With character, courage, and commitment, you can lead others through the courageous accountability process and celebrate success—all the while being an example of a growing leader.

THE NEXT GENERATION

Every generation has concerns about the following generations. Ours is no exception. However, changes in our cultural norms related to responsibility, accountability, and honor seem to have accelerated in the last fifty years at an ever increasing pace. But we desperately need the younger generations and they need us as good examples, especially as they come into the workplace. This is a challenge, but it's also a great opportunity to lay the groundwork for future success.

One thing we know about the younger generation is that they see through hypocrisy very quickly and push back on it hard. On the other hand, they are attracted by authenticity. Here is where the value of the personal, internal battle we've been talking about pays an extra dividend. Above and beyond your own growth and even the success of your team, your struggle to be authentic will be attractive and powerful. Your example can be exactly what they need to develop into the leaders who will soon fill our places and perhaps guide our society and lead our country.

Thank you for your willingness to engage with honor and build a culture of courageous accountability.

ENDNOTES

1   Here's how Asaph put it in Psalm 73. "But as for me, my feet were almost gone; my steps had well nigh slipped. For I was envious at the foolish, when I saw the prosperity of the wicked."

2   After the agreements were signed and while we were awaiting repatriation, our captors began giving us books that families had sent over the years. One that we read in my cell was Frankl's classic, *Man's Search for Meaning*. How powerful for me to read his account of life in the concentration camp while still sitting in a POW camp. It was an honor to meet Viktor Frankl and spend twenty minutes with him just two months after our release when he came to speak at the Univ. of Georgia. I re-read this book at least once every five years and highly recommend it.

3   Viktor E. Frankl, *Man's Search for Meaning*

Summary of Foot Stompers

Chapter 1

Honor is not automatic—it cannot be assumed. The strongest and most courageous leaders in history have fallen short. Everyday people like you and me are lying, stealing, cheating, and embezzling. You and I can win this battle if we truly believe that honor matters—and we are diligent to hold ourselves accountable. Our example will influence others—leadership always makes a difference.

Chapter 2

Honor is acquired by winning daily battles to overcome our ego and distorted self-interests. It can be "taught," but it's more likely "caught" from the example of those most influential in our lives—especially our leaders. Accountability requires a carrot and a stick; we need both to stay on course.

Chapter 3

Accountability is crucial to success. It requires leaders to go first, setting the example by their commitment to be responsible and accountable to themselves. Though human nature tends to resist it, accountability has many benefits, improving both individual and organizational performance. Accountability works best in a positive environment that focuses on three areas: (1) accomplishing the mission, (2) believing in and developing people, and (3) following through to ensure that responsibilities and commitments are carried out.

Chapter 4

Leaders go first and set the example for accountability. This requires a strong core of character, courage, and commitment. Be clear with yourself about your character by establishing your personal nonnegotiables. Then lean into the pain of your doubts and fears to do what you know is right. Don't forget to engage a team of peers to help you in this battle.

Chapter 5

Leaders clarify at every level from broad guidance to the specifics needed to do the work. Clarity ensures direction and standards. It shows the way and sets the boundaries and guardrails. Go the extra mile to make sure you and others have clarity at every level.

Chapter 6

Know yourself and coach yourself to do what you need to do to be a responsible, accountable leader. Remember—matching talents to task is critical to success. People are different and good leaders manage accordingly, recognizing individual talents and inspiring their people to succeed, while stretching them to develop to the next level.

Chapter 7

Effective leaders recognize that their people are human beings with a deep desire to be known, understood, valued, and appreciated. With this mindset, they intentionally connect with them to ensure inclusion, express appreciation, and show each individual his or her importance to the mission.

Chapter 8

Leading with courageous accountability requires a collaborative mindset toward working with people. Developing your team and guiding them to success is your primary responsibility. The payoff for this hard work is better results, higher morale, better engagement and retention, and next generation leaders who can take your place.

Chapter 9

Collaboration improves alignment and increases employee engagement. Be intentional and proactive. Take into account each individual's unique style and differences as you engage them with dialogue to support, encourage, evaluate, guide, correct, and give ongoing feedback. It will take courage at almost every step. Be courageous to do your duty, and you will be rewarded with loyal followers and ongoing success.

Chapter 10

Good leaders courageously celebrate individual and team successes. They recognize that celebrating is essential for good morale and employee engagement. They also courageously confront poor performance and hold themselves and others accountable—with clear consequences for poor performance, failed promises, broken commitments, and inappropriate behaviors. Failure to appropriately confront and hold people accountable is an abdication of responsibility that lowers standards, discourages good performers, and deprives poor performers of the consequences that can help them grow.

Photos provided by author

Appendix B
The Honor Code

HONOR CODE

This Honor Code was created to inspire leaders seeking to live with character, courage, and competence. These behaviors are the foundational principles for living and leading with honor.

1
Tell the truth, even when it's difficult.
Avoid duplicity and deceitful behavior.

2
Treat others with dignity and respect.
Take the lead, and show value to others.

3
Keep your word and your commitments.
Ask for relief sooner than later if necessary.

4
Be ethical.
Operate within the laws of the land, the guidelines of your profession, and the policies of your employer.

5
Act responsibly; do your duty, and be accountable.
Own your mistakes, and work to do better in the future.

6
Be courageous.
Lean into the pain of your fears to do what you know is right, even when it feels unnatural or uncomfortable.

7
Live your values.
Be faithful to your spiritual core, your conscience, and your deepest intuitions.

You can download a full-page color copy of the Honor Code at LeadingWithHonor.com.

Appendix C
Military Code of Conduct

I

I am an American, fighting in the forces which guard my country and our way of life. I am prepared to give my life in their defense.

II

I will never surrender of my own free will. If in command, I will never surrender the members of my command while they still have the means to resist.

III

If I am captured, I will continue to resist by all means available. I will make every effort to escape and aid others to escape. I will accept neither parole nor special favors from the enemy.

IV

If I become a prisoner of war, I will keep faith with my fellow prisoners. I will give no information or take part in any action which might be harmful to my comrades. If I am senior, I will take command. If not, I will obey the lawful orders of those appointed over me, and will back them up in every way.

V

When questioned, should I become a prisoner of war, I am required to give only name, rank, service number, and date of birth. I will evade answering further questions to the utmost of my ability. I will make no oral or written statements disloyal to my country and its allies or harmful to their cause.

VI

I will never forget that I am an American, fighting for freedom, responsible for my actions, and dedicated to the principles which made my country free. I will trust in my God and in the United States of America.

Appendix D
Resource List

*This list has been compiled to help you build your courageous account-
ability leadership style. Some of these resources are mentioned in this
book, while others are recommendations only.*

Accountability Book Resources:

Crucial Confrontations by Kerry Patterson, Joseph Grenny, Ron
McMillan, and Al Switzler

Courage: The Backbone of Leadership by Gus Lee with Diane Elliott-
Lee

*Decent People, Decent Company: How to Lead with Character at Work
and in Life* by Robert L. Turknett and Carolyn N. Turknett

Extreme Ownership: How U.S. Navy SEALS Lead and Win by Jocko
Willink and Leif Babin

*First Break All the Rules: What the World's Best Managers Do
Differently* by Marcus Buckingham and Curt Coffman

Hesselbein on Leadership by Frances Hesselbein

How the Mighty Fall: And Why Some Companies Never Give In by Jim
Collins

In Search of Excellence by Tom Peters

Leading with Honor by Lee Ellis

Leadership and Self-Deception: Getting out of the Box by The Arbinger
Institute

*No More Excuses: The Five Accountabilities for Personal and
Organizational Growth* by Sam Silverstein

*Non-Negotiable: The Story of Happy State Bank & The Power of
Accountability* by Sam Silverstein

The Advantage: Why Organizational Health Trumps Everything in Business by Patrick Lencioni

The Oz Principle: Getting Results Through Individual and Organizational Accountability by Roger Conners, Tom Smith, and Craig Hickman

The Power of Personal Accountability: Achieve What Matters to You by Mark Samuel & Sophie Chiche

The Six Fundamentals of Success: The Rules for Getting It Right for Yourself and Your Organization by Stuart R. Levine

Thoughts of a Philosophical Fighter Pilot by James Bond Stockdale

True North: Discover Your Authentic Leadership by Bill George with Peter Sims

Unaccountable: What Hospitals Won't Tell You and How Transparency Can Revolutionize Healthcare by Dr. Marin Makary

Accountability - Connecting and Collaborating Books:

Encouraging the Heart: A Leader's Guide to Rewarding and Recognizing Others by James M. Kouzes and Barry Z. Posner

How Full Is Your Bucket? by Tom Rath and Donald Clifton

Love Works: Seven Timeless Principles for Effective Leaders by Joel Manby

The Five Languages of Appreciation in the Workplace by Gary Chapman and Paul White

The Inspiration Factor: How You Can Revitalize Your Company Culture in 12 Weeks by Terry Barber with Pat Springle

Accountability Online Resources:

Find and Balance Your Leadership Tilt at LeadingWithHonor.com
(infographic)
Leadership Behavior DNA at LeadershipBehaviorDNA.com
(Assessment to learn your unique strengths and struggles and
those of your team members.)
Leading with Honor Assessment at LeadingWithHonor.com (free)
The Courage Challenge Card at LeadingWithHonor.com
The Honor Code document at LeadingWithHonor.com

Appendix E
The Courage Challenge
Checklist

Ultimately, the courage challenge in leadership is about freedom, and freedom is knowing yourself and being authentic—shedding away layers of protection that keep you from growing. Use this comparison list to identify areas that still need growth.

Freedom From:	Freedom To:
Being unsure of your best talents	Know and embrace your strengths and struggles
Being too focused on protecting and promoting yourself	√Identify and applaud the talents of others
Being rigid in your mindsets	Be open to change and growth
Micromanaging out of fear	Courageously empower and delegate to others
Being a leader who demands and dictates	Actively listen to the ideas and opinions of others
Leading from (or with) fear and anger	Lead from courage and confidence
A leadership style that is out of balance	Lead by getting results and building relationships
An "eggshell" environment that doesn't allow disagreement	Engage in healthy, creative conflict that gets buy-in
Managing everyone the same	Manage each person uniquely for greater success
Focusing mainly on personal goals	√Focus on team/organizational goals
End runs on other departments	Cooperate with peers and others
Assuming everyone gets it (or sees what I see)	Nail down clarity
Not confronting others	Confront others quickly and objectively

Appendix F
Courageous Accountability
Model - Executive Summary

This executive summary is provided for leaders to remove or copy from the book to reference on a daily basis.

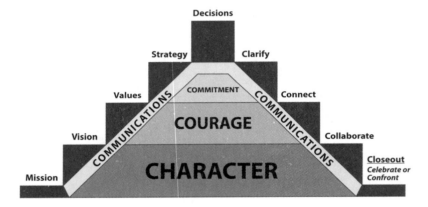

The Foundation of Courageous Accountability

Character
- ▶ Be aware (as a leader) of being held to a higher standard. You set the example that others will follow.
- ▶ Be confident yet humble.

Courage
- ▶ Lean into the pain of your doubts and fears to do what you know is right.

Commitment
- ▶ Dis-honorable behavior will corrode your will to move forward.
- ▶ Keep your promises and fulfill your obligations.
- ▶ Stay loyal to your values.

The Binding Agent of Courageous Accountability

Communications

▶ Be intentional about over-communicating important information and decisions.

▶ Don't assume that others think as you think or hear what you're really saying.

The 100,000 Foot View of Courageous Accountability

Mission

▶ Define the present state or purpose of your organization, and answer the questions, "Who are we?"; "What do we do?"; and "For whom do we do it?"

Vision

▶ Describe the desired future state of your organization 5-10 years from now.

Values

▶ Create a set of attributes and behaviors that define what is important to the organization and its members as they interact with each other and their stakeholders.

Strategy

▶ Plan the actions needed to bring about a desired future, such as achievement of a goal or solution to a problem.

Decisions

▶ Enact a set of conclusions, choices, or resolutions after consideration of the above steps.

The Courageous Accountability Model

Clarify

▶ Make sure that mission, vision, values, strategy, and choices are clear.

▶ Get alignment with your team or organization (in every level).

▶ Make sure that people understand what outcomes are expected, what resources are available, and what boundaries are in place.

▶ Solicit questions and listen to make sure people have the same picture you have. Reclarify until there is alignment.

Connect

▶ Know your and others' unique strengths, struggles, communication style, and results/relationships balance.

▶ Know how to uniquely manage each person.

▶ Connect with the heart by making people feel valued and important. Be vulnerable.

Collaborate

▶ Develop a proactive mindset about collaboration. Welcome and support it.

▶ Dialogue and provide ongoing feedback to encourage and correct.

▶ Remember to engage in collaboration rather than withdraw or dominate.

Closeout

▶ Celebrate successes.

▶ Confront problem issues with confidence and humility.

▶ Critique the process for continual improvement.

Appendix G
Pre-release Letter to
My Parents

12 MARCH 1973

Dearest Family,

I am hopeful that the next three days will bring silver wings to bear me safely back to the land of milk and honey, to freedom and a wonderful reunion with you. For you I know these many years have been very difficult and I regret that you have had to suffer so much. We have a saying here, "It's harder on them than it is on us," because for you there has been uncertainty, and many ups and downs. We have had faith and confidence in your welfare, but for you our situation was mostly unknown.

For me the years have passed rather rapidly and yet it seems that the first twenty-four years of my life were a dream or perhaps the experiences of a person whom I once knew. This has become a way of life and the world in which you have lived was a faraway thing. Yet at no time have I ever given up my faith in God, my family, my country and those things for which our heritage has always stood.

In the recent pictures that I have received you all look so healthy and fine. I can not tell you the pride and happiness this brings to me. I am so thankful that you have stood the years so well. You will be surprised I think to see my physical condition. My health has been good and I have no injuries. I have been very fortunate. I exercise six days a week and for the past three years I estimate my weight to have been one hundred and fifty pounds.

My mental health has fared quite well also. I think. Of course my only measure is my memory and a comparison of those within this closed society. I have matured and I think my judgement is better. I have learned more about responsibility and I think you will find me more indecisive. I have gained self-confidence and a deep sense of pride. By that I mean that if I do a job I want to do the best job possible, for to do less would bring dishonor upon myself and those who believe in me would be disappointed. I feel that I have learned a great deal about human nature from myself and those with whom I have lived so intimately these past years. I have learned patience and understanding and to try to do those things which should be done when the opportunity arises.

211

To imply that I have perfected these virtues would be far from the truth for I have not, nor shall I ever. But here lies the essence of my philosophy. To constantly work to improve in these areas and to always be correcting back to the course which I have charted for my life. I believe that happiness in life comes through achievement. Not just materialistic achievement but more specifically in the small victories gained from day to day in mans struggle to be the type of person which he feels he should be. This achievement not only brings honor to the man and his family, but more important it glorifies God. The last line of a poem which my roommate has just written sums up these ideas quite well, "More majestic monuments than men who live their faith can not be found". I hope that I have not sounded too egotistical nor philosophized too much, but I wanted to paint a picture of myself, granted it has been from my own eyes, so you could know what to expect.

With so little news these past years I have a tremendous curiosity as to the changes that have taken place in the family among friends and in society as a whole. I was quite shocked to hear about the divorces of two of my friends. I know that there will be many other sad bits of news and I have prepared myself to accept any and all possibilities. I hope you have a chronological list of all noteworthy events with which you can brief me. I have the feeling that many friends have done kindnesses for you during my absence and for this I am very grateful. Perhaps you could make a list of them for me.

There will be so many new things to see and learn and I have so many things that I want to do. I will be trying to make up for five and a half years, which is of course impossible, so I will have to resign my efforts to the high points.

212

Probably in all of History there have been few Uncles who were as proud of a nephew as I am of mine. He is certainly a fine looking lad and your reports on him have cheered me much. Yet that is what I would expect from such wonderful people as Robert and Pat. How proud I am of them and how much I look forward to seeing them again. I should say here that I am very proud of and grateful to all of my family.

I am sure that by now you have assimilated a list of eligible young ladies for me to date. Such a list might be beneficial and also somewhat humorous, especially since I am approaching thirty and some of the girls whom I will be dating were still in high school when I was shot down. Realizing that I have not sat in a chair, eaten with knife and fork at a table nor been in the presence of the fairer sex during all these years, I hope that you will plan a program of etiquette training for me. I feel sure that you have been given some guidelines as to how I should be treated, but please don't hesitate to criticize me. How else will I learn of my bad habits? I realize that there are many new things, ideas and ways of doing things and that I will be out of step with the times, perhaps even old-fashioned. My desire is to make a smooth transition and even now I have begun to wear my hair slightly longer.

At the present moment I would call my condition not excited but hopeful. The moment that I know I am a free man, safely in American hands, I shall be more excited and happy than I have ever been in my life. I look forward so much to seeing you and beginning to live a new life. May God grant that it will be soon. Wait for my call from Clarke and then we can plan our reunion. As yet I do not know what the agenda will be for me after release. Likewise, I am sure that it will be wonderful. Keep smiling.

All my love,
Lee

Appendix H
Courage Challenge and
Leadership Engagement Model

The Courage Challenge* is represented in the following statement:

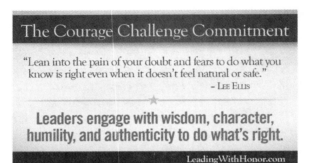

The Courage Challenge Commitment

"Lean into the pain of your doubt and fears to do what you know is right even when it doesn't feel natural or safe."
– LEE ELLIS

Leaders engage with wisdom, character, humility, and authenticity to do what's right.

LeadingWithHonor.com

Leadership Engagement Model™

WITHDRAW	*ENGAGE*	DOMINATE
• Retreat	• Believe	• Control
• Hide	• Initiate	• Dictate
• Avoid	• Dialogue	• Force
• Quit/Abandon	• Clarify	• Bully
• Go Passive/Aggressive	• Connect	• Manipulate
	• Collaborate	
	• Celebrate	
EMOTIONS:		*EMOTIONS:*
✓ Fear	*EMOTIONS:*	✓ Fear
✓ Anger	✓ *Courage*	✓ Anger
✓ Distrust	✓ *Respect/Love*	✓ Distrust
✓ Pride/Hubris	✓ *Trust*	✓ Pride/Hubris
✓ Pessimism	✓ *Humility*	✓ Pessimism
✓ Shame	✓ *Optimism*	✓ Shame
✓ Guilt	✓ *Self-respect*	✓ Guilt
	✓ *Confidence*	

*You may download or purchase copies of this card for your team at LeadingWithHonor.com.

Appendix I
Leadership Alignment Model

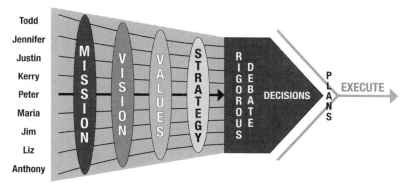

Leadership Alignment Model™
Clarify > Connect > Collaborate

In the Leadership Alignment Model shown above, you can see that any team has individuals with multiple talents, various experiences, and a depth and breadth of knowledge all coming together. Using this model, they can pull the issues of the organization through the lenses (or filters) of mission, vision, values, to form strategies or make decisions based on already existing strategies. These lenses serve as the guardrails acting like a funnel to help align these multiple talents and focus their collective skills and knowledge on the target issue under discussion. With good team-building they are able to build the trust and unity needed to have rigorous debate, (or courageous conflict) in order to make good decisions that can be executed with synergy to achieve important goals.

It's really about getting results to accomplishing the mission in the most effective way. At the same time, it's an efficient way to build on the "people" part of the ever-present need to take care of both mission and people.

Appendix J
Individual Courageous
Accountability Checklist

Name	John Doe	Jane Smith	Anthony Jackson
Photo			
Birthday			
Spouse Name			
Children's Name(s)			
Title			
Role			
Profile Type – Behavior Style*			
Strengths			
Struggles			
Current Projects			
Development Goals			
Courageous Accountability Checklist			
Encourage Character			
Model Courage			
Commitment			
Over-Communicate			
Clarify – Mission, Vision, Values			
Clarify Policies, Standards			
Clarify Tasks, Outcomes, Expectations			
Connect – Understand Behavior Style*			
Connect – Heart, Values, Purpose			
Collaborate – Dialogue, Listen			
Celebrate – Affirm, Reward			
Confront – Consequences			
Critique the Process			
Other			

Profile Type is referring to the Leadership Behavior Style from the Assessment Services available at LeadershipBehaviorDNA.com.

Acknowledgments

WRITING A BOOK may sound simple, but it's always a team effort and this one especially. I usually thank my wife Mary last, but this time I'm putting her first. You see I've been putting her second to my work for quite a while, especially while writing this book. She has been understanding and supportive all the way. In addition, she is an avid and discerning reader—the perfect partner for a writer. She has labored through many drafts of this book and her feedback is always on target. Thank you Mary for being a faithful partner, supporting my work and this book as we worked to make it a reality. I owe you—big time.

As with most everything I have done these last few years, the achievement of this book hinged on the planning and organization of Kevin Light, the Managing Director of FreedomStar Media. He knows how to get things done. Thanks Kevin for your faithful support.

Stormie Knight-Ellwanger books my speeches, interacts with our clients, coordinates with our endorsers and PR team, and schedules most everything I do. Thanks Stormie for your many contributions.

Editor Anne Alexander has served us extremely well, taking my rough manuscript and making it a readable book that we're proud of. Great job Anne.

For the layout on this book we rejoined with old friend Jim Armstrong. Great job Jim—thanks for saying "Yes." You were patient with us and fast with your response.

In the "back office" so to speak, Liz and Mindy take care of clients and keep the books. Thanks for setting me free to use my talents more effectively.

We're always grateful for our clients. By allowing us to serve you, you help us achieve our mission of developing leaders who develop leaders and spread our message about honor and accountability. We appreciate our strategic partner Hugh Massie and his team at DNA Behavior for their encouragement and support. Likewise we appreciate all our vendors, distribution and public relation partners, and media for their help in sharing the message.

I've been blessed over a lifetime with great friends, mentors, and connections—and now with "tribes" on social media. To you all, I say thank you for your many encouraging words and acts of support. In this group, a special thanks to several POW friends who came alongside to clarify and confirm stories and events for this book.

My family is small, but solid. My brother Robert and sister-in-law Pat are the best. They (along with our deceased parents) courageously carried on the fight for me and other POWs when we were all but forgotten in the camps. Thank you for making such a difference in our lives.

Finally, and most importantly, I'm thankful to my heavenly Father, my Lord, Jesus, and his Holy Spirit. You have guided, protected, and blessed me all the days of my life and I am so grateful. Your unconditional love continues to bring healing and freedom enabling me to grow toward the person you created me to be. Amen.

Index

INDEX

INDEX

About the Author

Lee Ellis is Founder and President of Leadership Freedom® LLC and FreedomStar Media®. He is an award-winning author, leadership consultant, and expert presenter in the areas of leadership, teambuilding, and human performance. His past clients include Fortune 500 senior executives and C-Level leaders in telecommunications, healthcare, military, and other business sectors. Some of his media appearances include interviews on networks such as CNN, CBS This Morning, C-SPAN, ABC World News, Fox News Channel, plus hundreds of engagements in various industry sectors throughout the world.

Lee served as an Air Force fighter pilot flying fifty-three combat missions over North Vietnam. In 1967 he was shot down and held as a POW for more than five years in Hanoi and surrounding camps. For his wartime service, he was awarded two Silver Stars, the Legion of Merit, the Bronze Star with Valor device, the Purple Heart, the Air Medal with eight Oak Leaf Clusters, and POW Medal. Lee resumed his Air Force career, serving in leadership roles of increasing responsibility including command of a flying squadron and leadership development organizations before retiring as a colonel.

Lee has a BA in History and a MS in Counseling and Human Development. He is a graduate of the Armed Forces Staff College and the Air War College. He has authored or co-authored five books on leadership and career development. Lee's last book entitled *Leading with Honor®: Leadership Lessons from the Hanoi Hilton* has received multiple awards since its release including Winner in the 2012 International Book Awards in the Business and Management Category, and selection on the 2013 U.S. Air Force Chief of Staff Reading List.

Lee and his wife Mary reside in the Atlanta, Georgia area and have four grown children and six grandchildren.

About the Foreword Author

Ralph de la Vega
Vice Chairman, AT&T Inc.
and Chief Executive Officer, AT&T Business
Solutions and AT&T International, LLC

Ralph de la Vega was appointed Vice Chairman of AT&T Inc. and CEO of Business Solutions & International on Feb. 1, 2016. He has overall responsibility for the company's integrated Business Solutions group which serves more than 3.5 million business customers in nearly 200 countries and territories, including nearly all of the world's Fortune 1000 companies. He also has overall responsibility for AT&T's wireless business operations in Mexico and DIRECTV in Latin America. He is also the author of the best-selling book *Obstacles Welcome: Turn Adversity to Advantage in Business and Life* (Thomas Nelson, 2009).

Leadership Development Services from Leading with Honor®

After reading *Engage with Honor*™, we recommend ongoing training to build upon the Courageous Accountability Model. We've trained some of the best leaders, teams, and organizations worldwide learn how to lead with character, courage, and commitment to drive better results and success.

By using content from *Leading with Honor*, *Engage with Honor*, and our behavioral assessment services from *Leadership Behavior DNA*™, our team uses a mix of learning styles and methodologies to maximize learning and retention such as –

- ▶ Traditional training instruction
- ▶ Team breakouts
- ▶ Large group Q&A and exercises
- ▶ Interactive visuals
- ▶ Printed training guides
- ▶ Various digital technology solutions

We create a custom learning process with each client to ensure that the training experience is remembered and applied.

Learn more at www.LeadingWithHonor.com

The Original Award-Winning Book from FreedomStar Media®

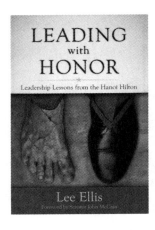

▶ *Publishers Weekly* calls *Leading with Honor* "moving" and "inspiring."

▶ *Foreword Reviews* says it is "provocative . . . an exceptionally well-constructed and well-written book."

▶ *Business Book Summaries* described it as "a gripping personal narrative" whose lessons will help leaders at all levels.

"In *Leading with Honor*, Lee draws from the POW experience, including some of his own personal story, to illustrate the crucial impact of leadership on the success of any organization. He highlights lessons and principles that can be applied to every leadership situation."

Senator John McCain
(Foreword excerpt – *Leading with Honor*)

How did American military leaders in the brutal POW camps of North Vietnam inspire their followers for six, seven, and even eight years to remain committed to the mission, resist a cruel enemy, and return home with honor? What leadership principles engendered such extreme devotion, perseverance, and teamwork?

In this award-winning powerful and practical book, Lee Ellis, a former Air Force pilot, candidly talks about his five and a half years of captivity and the 14 key leadership principles behind this amazing story.

To order: contact your favorite book retailer or visit www.LeadingWithHonor.com

Military, Businesses, and Industry Training Programs: contact www.FreedomStarMedia.com/Training for information on group training.